1

Acknowledgme

Information was taken from:-

- The Vital Guide to Modern Warshi|
  Ltd, Shrewsbury, 2001) ISBN 1 84(
- Seaforth World Naval Review 2010/15, edited by Conrad Waters.
  (Seaforth Publishing, Barnsley, S Yorkshire) ISBN 978 1 84832 051 2.
  ISBN 978 1 84832 075 8. ISBN 978 1 84832 120 5. ISBN 978 1 84832
  156 4. ISBN 978 1 84832 182 3. ISBN 978 1 84832 220 2.
- The World Encyclopedia of Amphibious Warfare Vessels. Bernard
  Ireland.(Lorenz Books, Anness Publishing Ltd, Blaby Road, Wigston
  Leicestershire LE18 4SE).
- The World Encyclopaedia of Military Helicopters. Francis Crosby.
  (Lorenz Books, Anness Publishing Ltd, Blaby Road, Wigston,
  Leicestershire LE18 4SE).
- The World Encyclopaedia of Fighters and Bombers. Francis Crosby.
  (Southwater books, Anness Publishing Ltd, Blaby Road, Wigston,
  Leicestershire LE18 4SE).
- The World Encyclopaedia of Destroyers, Frigates and Submarines.
  Bernard Ireland and John Parker. (Lorenz Books, Anness Publishing
  Ltd, Blaby Road, Wigston, Leicestershire LE18 4SE).
- The World Encyclopaedia of Aircraft Carriers and Naval Aircraft.
  Bernard Ireland and Francis Crosby. (Lorenz Books, Anness
  Publishing Ltd, Blaby Road, Wigston, Leicestershire LE18 4SE).
- The Encyclopaedia of Warships. Edited by Robert Jackson. (Thunder
  Bay Press, Advantage Publishers Group, 5880 Oberon Drive, San
  Diego, CA 92121-4794). ISBN-13: 978 1 59223 627 5. ISBN-10: 1
  59223 627 8.

THE MODERN GERMAN NAVY

INTRODUCTION

The German Navy, over the last one hundred years, has seen itself transformed several times. From the turn of the Twentieth Century to 1919, it was known as the Imperial German Navy. From 1919 to 1935, it was the Reichsmarine. From 1935 to 1945, it was the Kriegsmarine. After the Second World War, only a naval force for self-defence was allowed by the Allied Powers. This was known as the German Mine Sweeping Administration. It wasn't until 1956, that something close to the re-establishment of a German Navy began to take shape. Known as the Bundesmarine, it was part of the new West Germany, which was on the rise. It also helped to balance the forces between East and West, due to the Cold War. Finally, in 1995, after East and West Germany had reunited, did a proper navy come into being.
It is quite remarkable that the German people managed to keep their navy going, due to the massive expense of reunification. The German Navy is considered, in most circles, as somewhat of a small-to-medium force on the world stage. However, when you look at the number and types of vessels, which are in the German fleet, it certainly can hold its own against any naval fleet in the NATO Alliance.
The final two "Type 212" submarines have been delivered, bringing the force level up to six front line boats. It is also having some export success, with Poland possibly acquiring two boats.
The frigate force is still 'the teeth' of the German Navy. The "Bremen", "Brandenburg" and "Sachsen" classes are multi-purpose and powerful vessels, which have been kept up to date throughout their service lives. The "Bremen's" are starting to be withdrawn from service and are being replaced by a new type of frigate, which is designed for a new type of war. These are known as the "Baden-Wurttemberg" class. They are designed to deal with small local threats and not large-scale sea battles. The 'War on Terror' and Somali pirate actions are the main focus of these ships.
The fleet is moving towards deployments far from Germany in the Mediterranean Sea and East of Suez. More and more German vessels have been part of multi-national task groups heading into the Indian Ocean to help in coalition operations. Recent construction of long-range corvettes and more replenishment vessels have underlined this thinking.
The older patrol boats of the "Gepard" class are nearing the end of their service lives and will soon be replaced by a new design for operations in the North Sea and the Baltic Sea. Until recently, it was this type of vessel, which had to be deployed on long-range operations to fulfil Germany's obligations to the NATO Alliance. That is now, hopefully, a thing of the past.
The Mine Sweepers are coming to the end of their service lives and questions remain about whether they will be replaced or made to soldier on into the next decade, until a replacement class is available.
Despite a few unanswered questions, the German fleet isn't in bad shape, when you look at its obligations. It is more than capable of being part of any NATO or coalition operation for the foreseeable future.

Pennant Numbers

Ship	Pennant Number	Ship	Pennant Number
Submarines		**Minesweepers**	
U31	S181	Fulda	M1058
U32	S182	Weilheim	M1059
U33	S183	Rottweil	M1061
U34	S184	Sulzbach-Rosenberg	M1062
U35	S185	Bad Bevensen	M1063
U36	S186	Gromitz	M1064
		Dillingen	M1065
Frigates		Bad Rappenau	M1067
Niedersachsen	F208	Datteln	M1068
Karlsruhe	F212	Homburg	M1069
Augsburg	F213	Pegnitz	M1090
Lubeck	F214	Hameln	M1092
Brandenburg	F215	Auerbach/Oberpfalz	M1093
Schleswig-Holstein	F216	Ensdorf	M1094
Bayern	F217	Uberherrn	M1095
Mecklenburg-Vorpommern	F218	Sieburg	M1098
Sachsen	F219	Herten	M1099
Hamburg	F220		
Hessen	F221	**Minesweeper Drones**	
Baden-Wurttemberg*	F222	Seehund class	1-18
Nordrhein-Westfalen*	F223		
Sachsen-Anhalt*	F224	**Auxiliary Ships**	
Rheinland-Pfalz*	F225	Elbe	A511
		Mosel	A512
Corvettes		Rhein	A513
Braunschweig	F260	Werra	A514
Magdeburg	F261	Main	A515
Erfurt	F262	Donau	A516
Oldenburg	F263	Berlin	A1411
Ludwigshafen am Rhein	F264	Frankfurt am Main	A1412
		Bonn	A1413
Patrol Boats		Ammersee	A1425
Gepard	P6121	Tegernsee	A1426
Puma	P6122	Spessart	A1442
Hermelin	P6123	Rhon	A1443
Zobel	P6125		
Frettchen	P6126	**Surveillance Ships**	
Ozelot	P6128	Alster	A50
Wiesel	P6129	Oste	A52
Hyane	P6130	Oker	A53

*still under construction

Ship	Pennant Number	Ship	Pennant Number
Ocean-Going Tugboats		**Landing Craft**	
Wangerooge	A1451	Lachs	L762
Spiekeroog	A1452	Schlei	L765
Fehmarn	A1458		
		Research Ships	
Harbour Tugboats		Planet	A1437
Lutje Horn	Y812	Alliance	A1456
Knechtsand	Y814		
Scharhorn	Y815	**Trials Ships**	
Vogelsand	Y816	Kronsort	Y861
Norstrand	Y817	Helmsand	Y862
Langeness	Y819		
		Oil Recovery Ships	
Training Ships		Bottsand	A1643
Gorch Fork	A60	Eversand	A1644
Baltrum	A1439		
Juist	A1440		
Langeoog	A1441		

[2]"Naval Ensign"

Submarines

"Type 212" class

[3]"U34"

Bundeswehr-Fotos

Name	Pennant	Completed	Builder
U31	S181	2005	HDW
U32	S182	2005	HDW
U33	S183	2006	HDW
U34	S184	2007	HDW
U35	S185	2014	HDW
U36	S186	2014	HDW

Displacement. 1,830 tonnes   **Dimensions.** 56m x 7m x 6m
Speed. 20 knots   **Complement.** 27
Armament. 6 x 533mm torpedo tubes with 13 reloads; 24 mines; IDAS SAM's

Notes
This class of submarine is one of the most advanced diesel-electric submarines in the world. They have been designed and built as a joint project between Germany and Italy. The German Navy initially ordered four boats with the Italian Navy also ordering four boats. The Italian boats have been built by Fincantieri. Late into the program, the German Navy ordered two more boats, in 2006, with a slightly longer hull of 57 metres. Poland has announced that they wish to lease two "Type 212" boats instead of buying them. How they intend to do this is not quite clear. If they want to lease two new-build boats, what happens to them if after only a few years of

---
[3] Source http://commons.wikimedia.org/wiki/File:U_34_in_Fahrt.jpg

service they do not want them anymore? Do they just give them back to sit tied to a dock?

The design of these boats has been influenced by their need to operate in the confined and shallow waters of the Baltic Sea. This obviously doesn't affect the Italian boats, but they still choose them because of their long underwater endurance and technological advances. The hull is made of a non-magnetic material, which reduces the chance of being detected by magnetic mines. The planes have been arranged in an X position, which allows the boat to come closer to shore for surveillance operations.

The main weapon, as always, is their torpedoes of which thirteen are carried. Twenty-four mines can also be carried externally. In 2014, it is expected that the "IDAS" missile system will be deployed on these boats, giving them a surface-to-air capability. These missiles have a twenty-kilometre range and are fired from the torpedo tubes. Four such missiles can fit into one torpedo tube.

[4]"Type 212" in dock   (GFDL)

---

[4] Source http://commons.wikimedia.org/wiki/File:U_Boot_212_HDW_1.jpg

Frigates

"Sachsen" class

⁵"Hamburg"

US Navy/MCS Andrew Schneider

Name	Pennant	Completed	Builder
Sachsen	F219	2003	Blohm & Voss
Hamburg	F220	2004	HDW
Hessen	F221	2006	Nordseewerke

Displacement. 5,800 tonnes   **Dimensions.** 143m x 17.44m x 6m
Speed. 29 knots   **Complement.** 243
Armament. 1 x 76mm Oto Melara gun; 2 x 27mm Mauser autocannon;
        1 x Mk 41 VLS with 32 cells; 2 x RAM SAM CIWS; 8 x Harpoon SSM
        2 x triple torpedo tubes.
Aircraft. 2 x ASW helicopters

Notes
This class of frigate is currently the most advanced surface warship in the German
Navy and the world. Three vessels were initially ordered, with an option for a fourth.
This option, to date, has not been taken up. Rumours have recently emerged that
Israel intends to purchase two of these vessels, but this has yet to be confirmed. The
basic design is based on the "Brandenburg" class, but their size is that of a destroyer.
For the first time on a German warship, dedicated female quarters have been added.
They have been constructed to replace the old "Lutjens" class. They are armed with

---

5 Source http://commons.wikimedia.org/wiki/File:German_frigate_Hamburg_(F220)_in_the_Mediterranean_Sea_2013.jpg

a very balanced suite of short and long-range surface-to-air missiles, good anti-ship capability and a very good anti-submarine weapon suite.
Many have compared this class of ship to the Dutch "De Zeven Provincien" class. This is mainly due to the same Radar and surface-to-air missiles, which are carried. The 32 cell VLS is split between 24, SM-2 missiles, which is a long-range surface-to-air missile and 32 Evolved Sea Sparrow missiles, which is a medium-range missile. Each cell carries four missiles.
The helicopter landing deck and hangar, at the stern of the ship, is large enough to accommodate two helicopters of NH-90 size. These vessels can also act as flagships, with accommodation for an Admiral and thirteen of his staff.
These ships have a range of four thousand miles between refuelling, which has seen them operate further from Germany in combined task groups to either conduct operations in the Mediterranean Sea or East of Suez.

[6]"Hessen", top right, with US Navy   US Navy/MCS Gretchen M Albrecht

"Brandenburg" class

[7]"Bayern"   US Navy/MCS Mike Banzhaf

Name	Pennant	Completed	Builder
Brandenburg	F215	1994	Blohm & Voss
Schleswig-Holstein	F216	1995	HDW
Bayern	F217	1996	Nordseewerke
Mecklenburg-Vorpommern	F218	1996	Bremer Vulkan

Displacement. 3,600 tonnes   **Dimensions.** 138.85m x 15.7m x 4.35m
Speed. 29 knots   **Complement.** 219
Armament. 1 x 76mm Oto Melara gun; 2 x 27mm Mauser autocannon;
   1 x Mk 41 VLS with Evolved Sea Sparrow SAM; 2 x RAM SAM CIWS;
   4 x Exocet SSM; 4 x 324mm torpedo tubes
Aircraft. 2 x ASW helicopters

Notes
This class of multi-purpose frigate were designed to replace the "Hamburg" class frigates on a one-for-one basis. They have been designed on the modular theory. This is so each weapon system has its own box, which can be simply lifted out of the hull and replaced with an entirely new system that can plug into the existing wiring. This means that a vessel can be completed without its main armament and still put to

[7] Source http://commons.wikimedia.org/wiki/File:German_frigate_FGS_Bayern_F217.jpg

sea. This arrangement does look good on paper and has worked well in practise. The only drawback is that it requires a much larger ship's hull to carry these weapons than normal because the hull needs more strengthening although you do end up with a vessel, which can "take a beating" and still operate.

The weapon suite is therefore almost the same as the previous "Bremen" class frigate, but twenty-five percent more displacement. The Sea Sparrow SAM position has enough room available to double the number of Vertical Launch cells if required. Surprisingly, four Exocet anti-ship missiles were chosen instead of eight harpoons, which are deployed on the previous "Bremen" and following "Sachsen" class. Two "Super Lynx" helicopters are currently deployed, but whether these will be replaced by the "NH-90" helicopter remains to be seen.

[8]"Brandenburg"

Avalikarvamus

"Bremen" class

[9]"Lubeck"   Chris Bannister

Name	Pennant	Completed	Builder
Niedersachsen	F208	1982	AG Weser
Karlsruhe	F212	1984	HDW
Augsburg	F213	1989	Bremer Vulkan
Lubeck	F214	1990	Nordseewerke

Displacement. 3,680 tonnes   **Dimensions.** 130.5m x 14.6m x 6.3m
Speed. 30 knots   **Complement.** 222
Armament. 1 x 76mm Oto Melara gun; 2 x 27mm Mauser autocannon;
        1 x Octuple Sea Sparrow SAM; 2 x RAM SAM CIWS;
        8 x Harpoon SSM; 4 x 324mm torpedo tubes
Aircraft. 2 x ASW helicopters

Notes
The "Bremen" class are the German ships of an international program with the Dutch to build an anti-submarine frigate. Eight German vessels were built and ten Dutch. The Dutch vessels are the "Kortenaer" class. The German ships were the replacements for the "Fletcher" type119 class of destroyers and the "Koln" type 120 class of frigates. Each of the five shipyards involved in this program constructed its vessel/vessels and it was then towed to the Bremer Vulkan yard for the final fitting out of electronics and weapon systems.
The weapon suite is based mainly on US systems and the propulsion is the Fiat built, American LM 2500 turbines. These ships are the last in the German Navy to have

[9] Source http://commons.wikimedia.org/wiki/File:F214-L%C3%BCbeck-Plymouth_Sound.jpg

weight restrictions placed upon them due to post war sanctions. Midlife modernizations began in the 1990s with a full electronic update and the adding of the Rolling Airframe Missile system to each stern corner, above the helicopter hangar. Two "Sea Lynx" anti-submarine helicopters are carried. These can also be armed with air launched anti-ship missiles.

By the year 2010, it was considered not practical to modify these vessels any further and they began to be withdrawn from service. "Koln F211" was the first to go in 2012, followed by "Emden F210" and "Rheinland-Pfalz F209" in 2013. The lead ship "Bremen F207" was decommissioned in 2014.

The "Bremen's" will be replaced by the new type 125 class of frigate from the year 2016 onwards.

[10]"Niedersachsen" in New York   US Navy/Steven J Weber

[10] Source http://commons.wikimedia.org/wiki/File:F208_Niedersachsen.jpg

"Baden-Wurttemberg" class

"Baden-Wurttemberg"[11]

Bundesstefan

Name	Pennant	Completed	Builder
Baden-Wurttemberg	F222	Expected 2017	ThyssenKrupp
Nordrhein-Westfalen	F223	Expected 2017	Lurssen, Bremen
Sachsen-Anhalt	F224	Expected 2018	ThyssenKrupp
Rheinland-Pfalz	F225	Expected 2019	Lurssen, Bremen

Displacement. 7,200 tonnes   **Dimensions.** 149.52m x 18.8m x 5m
Speed. 26 knots   **Complement.** 190
Armament. 1 x 127mm Otobreda gun; 2 x 27mm Mauser autocannon;
    2 x RAM SAM CIWS; 8 x Harpoon SSM; 2 x 12.7mm Machine guns;
    5 x 12.7mm Hitrole gun turrets
Aircraft. 2 x ASW helicopters

Notes
These new vessels are the largest warships in the world to be classified as frigates. They will replace the "Bremen" class frigates. The whole concept of these vessels differs vastly from previous designs. They are designed to operate far from Germany in trouble spots such as the Horn of Africa where the normal high-level threats from submarines and aircraft have been replaced by small fast moving motorboats or skiffs, with lightly armed crews. This is why only short-range point defence weapons will be installed and no anti-submarine capability. Non-lethal systems have been added, such as water cannon and searchlights. These vessels have however, been designed on a modular scale, so they can be rearmed for conventional warfare if the situation calls for it. Service introduction was to have been between 2016/2018. Problems in construction of the first ship have pushed initial service entry to, maybe 2017, with a knock-on effect for the following vessels.

---

[11] Source https://commons.wikimedia.org/wiki/File:F222_-_Baden-W%C3%BCrttemberg.JPG?uselang=en-gb

Corvettes

"Braunschweig" class

[12]"Braunschweig"   Ein Dahmer

Name	Pennant	Completed	Builder
Braunschweig	F260	2008	Blohm & Voss
Magdeburg	F261	2008	Lurssen-Werft
Erfurt	F262	2013	Nordseewerke
Oldenburg	F263	2013	Blohm & Voss
Ludwigshafen am Rhein	F264	2013	Lurssen-Werft

Displacement. 1,840 tonnes   **Dimensions.** 89.12m x 13.28m x 3.4m
Speed. 26 knots   **Complement.** 65
Armament. 1 x 76mm Otobreda gun; 2 x 27mm Mauser autocannon;
        2 x RAM SAM CIWS; 4 x RBS-15 SSM

Notes
This class of corvette has been constructed to supplement the "Gepard" class of patrol boat. These vessels are another example of the German Navy building larger vessels with more range and capability to operate further from Germany in support of NATO and coalition operations.

These vessels are class as corvettes but they have been given pennant numbers of frigates. Their weapon suite is that of a light frigate also, but without the anti-submarine element. A large flight deck at the stern of the ships has been provided to take a helicopter of "NH-90" size, but the hangar is only large enough to deploy the "Camcopter S-100" helicopter drone.

Their anti-ship and anti-aircraft armament is considerable for such a small ship and with a range of four thousand miles; operations East of Suez are more than possible. There is however, no funnel, which is unusual for a ship of this size, but this does reduce the infrared signature of these vessels by a large amount. The ship's smoke exits just above the water line, amidships on both sides. This does however; leave a very dirty black mark on the hull, which has lead to that section of the hull being painted black to try to hide it.

Problems during construction have delayed the service entry of these vessels by about five years. Five years have lapsed since the commissioning of the second vessel to the third. Difficulties with the new lightweight gears have been the reason for this delay.

[13]"Ludwigshafen am Rhein"   Ein Dahmer

---

[13] Source http://commons.wikimedia.org/wiki/File:LUDWIGSHAFEN_3430.jpg?uselang=en-gb

Fast Patrol Boats

"Gepard" class

[14]"Frettchen"   Bundeswehr-Fotos

Name	Pennant	Completed	Builder
Gepard	P6121	1982	Kroger Werft
Puma	P6122	1983	Kroger Werft
Hermelin	P6123	1983	Kroger Werft
Zobel	P6125	1983	Kroger Werft
Frettchen	P6126	1983	Kroger Werft
Ozelot	P6128	1984	Kroger Werft
Wiesel	P6129	1984	Kroger Werft
Hyane	P6130	1984	Kroger Werft

Displacement. 390 tonnes   **Dimensions.** 57.6m x 7.8m x 2.6m
Speed. 40 knots   **Complement.** 36
Armament. 1 x 76mm Otobreda gun; 2 x 12.7mm Machine guns
                    1 x RAM SAM CIWS; 4 x Exocet SSM

Notes
These are the only class of fast patrol boats in service with the German Navy. This
class of fast patrol boats originally numbered ten. The "Nerz P6124" and "Dachs
P6127" were decommissioned in 2012 and transferred to Ghana.

---

[14] Source http://commons.wikimedia.org/wiki/File:Schnellboot_Gepard-Klasse_Typ_143_A.jpg

They are based on the "Albatross" class of patrol except instead of a second 76mm gun there is now a RAM surface-to-air missile system. For their size, these vessels are very well armed compared to vessels of the same size in service with other nations. With the introduction of more advanced and longer-range vessels to the German fleet, these ships can operate closer to Germany instead of further afield as these have had to do, to keep up Germany's commitment to NATO operations, mainly in the Mediterranean Sea. It is planned that these vessels will serve into the next decade and then be replaced by a new design of patrol boat.

[15]"Gepard"   user: yetdark

Minesweepers

"Ensdorf" class

[16]"Hameln"   Lung(?)

Name	Pennant	Completed	Builder
Ensdorf	M1094	1990	Lurssen
Auerbach/Oberpfalz	M1093	1991	Lurssen
Hameln	M1092	1989	Lurssen
Pegnitz	M1090	1990	Lurssen
Sieburg	M1098	1990	Kroger Werft

Displacement. 650 tonnes   **Dimensions.** 54.4m x 9.2m x 2.84m
Speed. 18 knots   **Complement.** 45
Armament. 2 x Mauser 27mm autocannon

Notes
These minesweepers are part of an original class of twenty-two vessels, which were built to replace older "Lindau" class of minesweepers, which were constructed in the late 1950's. They were built at the height of the Cold War to replace up to sixty vessels of various classes in total. Most of the "Lindau" ships were transferred to friendly countries.
These five ships started their service lives classed as "Type 343" minesweepers. Between the years 1999 and 2001, they were modernized to a higher standard so they would be classified as "Type 352". It is expected that all the vessels in this class will be out of service by the end of 2015.

---

[16] Source http://commons.wikimedia.org/wiki/File:M1092_0111.jpg?uselang=en-gb

The original armament of two "40mm Bofors" have been replaced by two "27mm Mauser" autocannons. They also have a considerable mine laying capability with up to sixty mines being able to be carried and deployed. These vessels use the unusual method of mine detection and disposal by deploying remotely controlled boats to explode the mines like a normal ship would if it encountered the mine. These boats are however, capable of surviving the detonation and continuing to the next target.

[17]"Hameln" HeidlmFeld

[17] Source https://commons.wikimedia.org/wiki/File:FGS-Hameln.jpg?uselang=en-gb

Minesweepers

"Ensdorf" class

[16]"Hameln"   Lung(?)

Name	Pennant	Completed	Builder
Ensdorf	M1094	1990	Lurssen
Auerbach/Oberpfalz	M1093	1991	Lurssen
Hameln	M1092	1989	Lurssen
Pegnitz	M1090	1990	Lurssen
Sieburg	M1098	1990	Kroger Werft

Displacement. 650 tonnes   **Dimensions.** 54.4m x 9.2m x 2.84m
Speed. 18 knots   **Complement.** 45
Armament. 2 x Mauser 27mm autocannon

Notes
These minesweepers are part of an original class of twenty-two vessels, which were built to replace older "Lindau" class of minesweepers, which were constructed in the late 1950's. They were built at the height of the Cold War to replace up to sixty vessels of various classes in total. Most of the "Lindau" ships were transferred to friendly countries.
These five ships started their service lives classed as "Type 343" minesweepers. Between the years 1999 and 2001, they were modernized to a higher standard so they would be classified as "Type 352". It is expected that all the vessels in this class will be out of service by the end of 2015.

---

[16] Source http://commons.wikimedia.org/wiki/File:M1092_0111.jpg?uselang=en-gb

"Frankenthal" class

[19]"Gromitz"

Thomas Glapa

Name	Pennant	Completed	Builder
Fulda	M1058	1998	Abeking & Rasmussen
Weilheim	M1059	1998	Lurssen
Rottweil	M1061	1993	Lurssen
Sulzbach-Rosenberg	M1062	1996	Lurssen
Bad Bevensen	M0163	1993	Lurssen
Gromitz	M1064	1994	Kroger Werft
Dillingen	M1065	1995	Abeking & Rasmussen
Bad Rappenau	M1067	1994	Abeking & Rasmussen
Datteln	M1068	1994	Lurssen
Homburg	M1069	1995	Kroger Werft

Displacement. 644 tonnes
Speed. 18 knots
Armament. 2 x Mauser 27mm autocannon

Dimensions. 54.4m x 9.2m x 2.6m
Complement. 42

[19] Source http://commons.wikimedia.org/wiki/File:Minenjagdboot_Gr%C3%B6mitz.JPG

Notes
These minesweepers are part of an original class of twenty-two vessels, which were built to replace older "Lindau" class of minesweepers, which were constructed in the late 1950's. They were built at the height of the Cold War to replace up to sixty vessels of various classes in total. Most of the "Lindau" ships were transferred to friendly countries. They represent part of the third generation of minesweepers/hunters for the German Navy. These vessels were built from the outset as mine hunters and not converted like the "Kulmbach" and "Ensdorf" classes. Not only can they hunt and destroy mines, they can also scan the seabed for objects and map the seabed.
They are equipped with the "Penguin" mine-hunting drone and can also deploy divers. A decompression is also embarked.
In 2006 the lead vessel. "Frankenthal M1066" and "Weiden M1060" were transferred to the United Arab Emirates.

[20]"Datteln"

Ein Dahmer

---

[20] Source http://commons.wikimedia.org/wiki/File:DATTELN_6982.jpg?uselang=en-gb

Mine Sweeping Drones

"Seehund" class

[21]"Seehund" Drones   de:Benutzer: Gonagal

Name	Pennant	Completed	Builder
	1	1981	Burmester Werft ?
	2	1981	Burmester Werft ?
	3	1981	Burmester Werft ?
	4	1982	Burmester Werft ?
	5	1982	Burmester Werft ?
	6	1982	Burmester Werft ?
	7	1981	Burmester Werft ?
	8	1981	Burmester Werft ?
	9	1981	Burmester Werft ?
	10	1981	Burmester Werft ?
	11	1981	Burmester Werft ?
	12	1981	Burmester Werft ?
	13	1982	Burmester Werft ?
	14	1982	Burmester Werft ?
	15	1982	Burmester Werft ?
	16	1983	Burmester Werft ?
	17	1983	Burmester Werft ?
	18	1983	Burmester Werft ?

---

[21] Source http://commons.wikimedia.org/wiki/File:SeehundeTroika.jpg?uselang=en-gb

Displacement. 91 tonnes
Speed. 9.5 knots

Dimensions. 25m x 4 46m x 1.8m
Complement. 3

Notes

These small boats are minesweeping drones, which are controlled by a "mother ship". When they are under independent control, they have a crew of three. These men are taken off the ship when minesweeping begins. When a drone finds a mine it detonates it itself. These boats are designed to survive the explosion and then proceed to the next mine.

The entire system is called "Seehund Troika". The hull is made from wood with a metal inner core. Unfortunately, information on these vessels is very hard to come by and it is assumed that Burmester Werft constructed these boats, as they were the builders of the old "Lindau" class of minesweeper that these boats were originally assigned. This also makes these drones older than their present minesweeper "mother ships". The "Seehund" system will soon be replaced by the "Seepferd" system.

Drones 1, 2, 3 and 11 are assigned to the "Hameln. Drones 4, 5 and 6 are assigned to the "Auerbach/Oberfalz". Drones 7, 8, 9 and 10 are assigned to the "Sieburg. Drones 12, 13, 14 and 15 are assigned to the "Pegnitz". Drones 16, 17 and 18 are assigned to the "Ensdorf".

[22]"Hameln" and drones

mattbuck

---
[22] Source
http://commons.wikimedia.org/wiki/File:London_MMB_%C2%BB0S7_City_Canal_and_Deutsche_Marine.jpg?uselang=en-gb

Replenishment Oiler

"Berlin" class

Ein Dahmer

Name	Pennant	Completed	Builder
Berlin	A1411	2001	Flensburger Schiffbau-Gesellschaft
Frankfurt am Main	A1412	2002	Flensburger Schiffbau-Gesellschaft
Bonn	A1413	2013	Flensburger Schiffbau-Gesellschaft

Displacement. 20,240 tonnes   **Dimensions.** 173.7m x 24m x 7.6m
Speed. 20 knots   **Complement.** 139
Armament. 4 x Mauser 27mm autocannon
Aircraft. 2 x Medium helicopters

Notes
These three auxiliary vessels are the largest ships in the German Navy. This class was originally only two ships, "Berlin" and "Frankfurt am Main". In 2013, a third ship was commissioned, "Bonn", to ease the navy's replenishment requirements due to longer deployments of warships to the Mediterranean Sea and East of Suez in support of international operations. "Bonn" was built by a consortium of builders and not just one yard.

---

[23] Source http://commons.wikimedia.org/wiki/File:BERLIN_2268.jpg?uselang=en-gb

These ships carry diesel fuel, ammunition, dry stores and fresh water to resupply ships at sea. Two medium sized helicopters are permanently embarked to aid in resupply and search and rescue operations.

Full medical facilities are onboard to treat up to forty-five patients. These facilities can be augmented by using the helicopter hangar to house more patients.

Exports of this design of vessel have been very successful, with Canada announcing that it will have two of these vessels constructed for the Royal Canadian Navy.

[24]"Bonn"

euscho

[24] Source http://commons.wikimedia.org/wiki/File:Versorger_Bonn_A1413_in_der_Flensburger_F%C3%B6rde_-_Bb_achtern.png?uselang=en-gb

"Rhon" class

25"Rhon"

Mark Harkin

Name	Pennant	Completed	Builder
Rhon	A1443	1974	Kroger, Rendsburg
Spessart	A1442	1974	Kroger, Rendsburg

Displacement. 14,169 tonnes

Speed. 16 knots

Dimensions. 130.2m x 19.3m x 8.2m

Complement. 42

Notes

These two auxiliary oilers were originally order by Libya, but were acquired by the German Navy in 1977 after the contract fell through.

They carry mainly diesel fuel for transfer at sea. Both ships have operated East of Suez in support of international operations, involving the war on terror and off the Horn of Africa against Somali pirates.

Coastal Tanker

"Walchensee" class

[26]"Tegernsee"   KuK

Name	Pennant	Completed	Builder
Ammersee	A1425	1967	Lindenau-Werft
Tegernsee	A1426	1967	Lindenau-Werft

Displacement. 2,174 tonnes
Speed. 12.5 knots

Dimensions. 74.2m x 11.22m x 4.54m
Complement. 21

Notes

This was originally a class of four vessels. "Walchensee A1424" was decommissioned in 2001 and sold. In 2003, "Westensee A1427" was decommissioned and scrapped. The two remaining ships transport fuel and other liquid stores between depots and ports.

These two vessels are showing their age and will soon be decommissioned.

---

[26] Source http://commons.wikimedia.org/wiki/File:Tegernsee_1.JPG?uselang=en-gb

Tenders

"Elbe" class

[27] "Elbe"   US Navy/Mike Banzhaf

Name	Pennant	Completed	Builder
Elbe	A511	1993	Bremer Vulkan
Mosel	A512	1993	Bremer Vulkan
Rhein	A513	1993	Flensburger Schiftbau
Werra	A514	1993	Flensburger Schiftbau
Main	A515	1994	Kroger Werft
Donau	A516	1994	Kroger Werft

Displacement. 3,586 tonnes   **Dimensions.** 100.55m x 15.4m x 4.05m
Speed. 15 knots   **Complement.** 40
Armament. 2 x 27mm Mauser autocannon

Notes
This class of replenishment ships are often referred to as "Tenders" because they were built to support submarines and squadrons of small surface vessels. The "Main" has been refitted primarily to support submarines.

As tenders, they carry everything a warship needs, such as fuel, ammunition, fresh water and dry stores. Repair and medical facilities are also on board, therefore, these vessels can in theory, anchor and be used as a forward base. There is also an extensive command and control suite embarked so that these vessels can act as flagships, if necessary. A waste disposal facility is also onboard.

The fore deck is large enough to take specialised containers to support different types of vessels. There is a large helicopter pad at the stern, but no hangar or support facilities are embarked.

[28]"Rhein"

Pelz

Surveillance Ships

"Oste" class

[29]"Alster"

Bin im Garten

Name	Pennant	Completed	Builder
Alster	A50	1989	Flensburger Schiffbau-Gesellschaft
Oste	A52	1988	Flensburger Schiffbau-Gesellschaft
Oker	A53	1988	Flensburger Schiffbau-Gesellschaft

Displacement. 3,200 tonnes   **Dimensions.** 83.5m x 14.6m x 4.2m
Speed. 21 knots   **Complement.** 36

Notes
These vessels are the German Navy's intelligence gathering ships. They were originally built to spy on Soviet Naval forces in the North Atlantic and the Baltic Sea. They carry the most modern electro-optic, electromagnetic and hydro-acoustic equipment for intelligence gathering. They can listen in on telephone and radio communications and pinpoint radar locations. She can also act as an early warning station. Their crew's can be augmented by forty mission specialists.
Since the end of the Cold War, these vessels have operated further away from Germany, mainly in the Mediterranean Sea and sometimes East of Suez.

---

[29] Source http://commons.wikimedia.org/wiki/File:Hafen_Kiel_2010_PD_016.JPG?uselang=en-gb

Ocean-Going Tugs

"Helgoland" class

[30]"Fehmarn"

Gerhard kemme

Name	Pennant	Completed	Builder
Fehmarn	A1458	1967	Unterweser Bremerhaven

Displacement. 1,310 tonnes   **Dimensions.** 68m x 12.7m x 4.4m
Speed. 16.6 knots   **Complement.** 45

Notes
This was originally a class of two ocean-going tugboats. The lead boat, "Helgoland", was decommissioned in 1997 and sold to Uruguay.
This tugboat is manned by a civilian crew and is used for basic towing of ships in trouble or towing target vessels. She is capable of ice breaking and fire fighting if necessary. She can also participate in salvage operations.

---

[30] Source http://commons.wikimedia.org/wiki/File:Bergungsschlepper_Fehmarn_A1458.jpg?uselang=en-gb

"Wangerooge" class

[31]"Wangerooge"

Ein Dahmer

Name	Pennant	Completed	Builder
Wangerooge	A1451	1968	Unterweser Bremerhaven
Spiekeroog	A1452	1968	Unterweser Bremerhaven

Displacement. 798 tonnes
Speed. 12 knots

Dimensions. 52.7m x 12.2m x 4.2m
Complement. 33

Notes
This was originally a class of six ocean-going tugboats. Only "Wangerooge" and "Spiekeroog" are still in service as tugboats. "Norderney" was decommissioned in 1970 and transferred to Uruguay. "Langeoog", "Baltrum" and "Juist" have all been refitted and act as training vessels.
The main duties of these vessels are towing maritime shipping, target towing and marine salvage.

---

[31] Source http://commons.wikimedia.org/wiki/File:WANGEROOGE_1889.jpg?uselang=en-gb

Harbour Tugboats

"Nordstrand" class

[32]"Knechtsand"

Ein Dahmer

Name	Pennant	Completed	Builder
Norstrand	Y817	1987	Orenstein & Koppel
Langeness	Y819	1987	Orenstein & Koppel
Vogelsand	Y816	1987	Orenstein & Koppel
Lufje Horn	Y812	1990	Husumer Schiffswerft
Scharhorn	Y815	1990	Husumer Schiffswerft
Knechtsand	Y814	1990	Husumer Schiffswerft

Displacement. 278 tonnes
Speed. 12 knots

Dimensions. 30.25m x 9.1m x 2.55m
Complement. 10

Notes
Twelve vessels of this class were originally ordered. The final six were later cancelled. They have replaced tugboats with the same names, which were built in 1959. These tugs can be seen at the major naval ports of Germany.

---

[32] Source http://commons.wikimedia.org/wiki/File:KNECHTSAND_2271.jpg

Landing Craft

"Barbe" class

³³"Lachs"

Tim Becker

Name	Pennant	Completed	Builder
Lachs	L762	1966	Howaldtswerke
Schlei	L765	1966	Howaldtswerke

Displacement. 403 tonnes   **Dimensions.** 40.04m x 8.8m x 2.01m
Speed. 12 knots   **Complement.** 17
Armament. 2 x 20mm guns

Notes
This class of landing craft, originally numbered, twenty-two. Only "Lachs" and "Schlei" remain active. "Flunder L760", "Plotze L763" and "Zander L769" have been decommissioned. "Butt L788", "Brasse L789", "Karpfen L761", "Stor L766", "Tummler L767" and "Wels L768" have been scrapped. "Renke L798" and "Salm L799" were decommissioned in 1988 and transferred to Greece. "Barbe L790", "Delphin L791", "Dorsch L792", "Felchen L793", "Florelle L794", "Inger L795" and "Makrele L796" were decommissioned in 1991 and went to Greece. "Rochen L764" and "Murane L797" were decommissioned in 1992 and went Greece.

---

³³ Source http://www.shipspotting.com/gallery/photo.php?lid=890543

These boats were designed to operate in the North and Baltic Seas in support of German ground forces. They can transport three heavy tanks or 170 tonnes of other stores. Their bow and stern ramps allow them to act as pontoons if necessary. It is expected that the final two vessels will be decommissioned soon and be replaced by a new class of landing craft.

[34]"Schlei"

Frank Schlunsen

Oil Recovery Ships

"Bottsand" class

[35]"Bottsand"

Ralf Roletschek/fahrradmonteur.de

Name	Pennant	Completed	Builder
Bottsand	Y1643	1984	C, Luhring Schiffswerft
Eversand	Y1644	1987	Brake & Hegemann

Displacement. 650 tonnes   **Dimensions.** 46.3m x 12m x 3.1m
Speed. 10 knots   **Complement.** 6

Notes
These ships were built for the purpose of anti-pollution. The vessel is hinged at the stern, allowing the entire vessel to open into a "V" shape to allow the polluted water to pass through and be collected in the ship's tanks. It is then treated and the clean water is pumped back into the sea. Up to 140 square metres of ocean can be cleaned every hour.

---

[35] Source https://commons.wikimedia.org/wiki/File:13-08-21-marinest%C3%BCtzpunktkommando-kiel-086.jpg?uselang=en-gb

Diver Training Ships

"Wangerooge" class

[36]"Baltrum"   Ein Dahmer

Name	Pennant	Completed	Builder
Baltrum	A1439	1968	Unterweser Bremerhaven
Juist	A1440	1968	Unterweser Bremerhaven
Langeoog	A1441	1971	Unterweser Bremerhaven

Displacement. 798 tonnes
Speed. 12 knots

Dimensions. 52.7m x 12.2m x 4.2m
Complement. 33

Notes

These vessels are part of the "Wangerooge" class of ocean-going tugboats. These three ships were refitted to act as training vessels for navy divers. Survival training for aircrews has also carried out onboard ship.

---

[36] Source http://commons.wikimedia.org/wiki/File:BALTRUM_1633.jpg?uselang=en-gb

Training Ship

"Gorch Fork"

[37]"Gorch Fock"   Felix Koenig

Name	Pennant	Completed	Builder
Gorch Fock	A60	1958	Blohm & Voss

Displacement. 1,760 tonnes   **Dimensions.** 81.2m x 12m x 5.2m
Speed. 18 knots   **Complement.** 222

Notes
This vessel was built to replace the original "Gorch Fork", which was taken by the Russians at the end of World War 2, as war reparations. This ship was built to a modified design and has been the German Navy's main training vessel for midshipman ever since. Many refer to her as the "Gorch Fork 2".
She participates in most of the tall ship events around the world, in company with tall ships of other navies. Sometimes as many as six of these fine vessels can be seen in close company, on round-the-world cruises.

---

[37] Source http://commons.wikimedia.org/wiki/File:Gorch_Fock_unter_Segeln_Kieler_Foerde_2006.jpg

Research Ship

"Planet" class

[38]"Planet"

Klugschnacker

Name	Pennant	Completed	Builder
Planet	A1437	2003	Nordseewerke

Displacement. 3,500 tonnes **Dimensions.** 73m x 27.2m x 6.8m
Speed. 15 knots **Complement.** 20

Notes
This vessel is one of the most modern research ships in the world. It is built on the
SWATH design, which is a catamaran type hull, but instead of it riding on the surface,
most of the torpedo shaped hulls is beneath the surface. This gives a very stable
platform for crews to work. She is equipped with various technologies, which are
under development, including new torpedo systems. Beside the crew, an extra
twenty scientists can be embarked for weapon trials.

[38] Source http://commons.wikimedia.org/wiki/File:Wehrforschungsschiff_PLANET_vor_der_Stralsunder_VOLKSWERFT_(2008-05-11).JPG

"Alliance" class

[39]"Alliance"

VollwertBIT

Name	Pennant	Completed	Builder
Alliance	A1456	1988	Fincantieri

Displacement. 2,920 tonnes
Speed. Approx 16 knots

Dimensions. 93m x 15.2m x 5.2m
Complement. 24

Notes
This research vessel is assigned to NATO, but is operated under the German Navy.
The captain and senior crew are German, but most of the other crew are either
British or Italian.
The ship's main duties are maritime research and experimentation. There is a very
large laboratory aboard with accommodation for up to twenty-four scientific
personnel. It can survey and retrieve objects from the seabed if necessary. This also
enables this vessel to participate in salvage operations.

---

[39] Source http://commons.wikimedia.org/wiki/File:Alliance_Kiel2008.jpg

Multi-Purpose Trials Ships

"Schwedeneck" class

[40]"Kronsort"

Malte Classens

Name	Pennant	Completed	Builder
Kronsort	Y861	1987	Elsflether Werft
Helmsand	Y862	1988	Elsflether Werft

Displacement. 850 tonnes
Speed. 12.6 knots

Dimensions. 54.5m x 11m x 3.7m
Complement. 13

Notes

This was originally a class of three trials ships for the German Navy. In 2011, the lead ship "Schwedeneck Y860", was decommissioned and transferred to civilian use. These ships carry out weapon testing and various other equipment-under-development for the navy. Up to ten scientists can be embarked for such trials.

---

[40] Source http://www.shipspotting.com/gallery/photo.php?lid=940520

Naval Aviation

"P-3C Orion"

[41]"P-3C"

Bthebest

Role. Maritime patrol aircraft
Engines. 4 x Allison T56-A-14 turboprops
Length. 35.6m   **Wingspan.** 30.4m   **Height.** 11.8m
Max Weight. 64,400 kgs   **Range.** 4,400 kms
Max Speed. 750 km/h   **Service Ceiling.** 28,300 feet
Crew. 11
Avionics. Raytheon AN/APS-115 Maritime Surveillance Radar, AN/APS-137D(V)5 Inverse Synthetic Aperture Search Radar. IFF: APX-72: APX-76: APX-118/123 Interrogation Friend or Foe (IFF). EO/IR: ASX-4 Advanced Imaging Multispectral (AIMS), ASX-6 Multi-Mode Imaging System (MMIS)
Armament. 20,000lbs of torpedoes, bombs, sonobuoys etc

Notes
This type of aircraft first flew in 1958. Its mission is primarily Maritime Reconnaissance, but it is also able to track and engage surface and sub-surface targets with a wide variety of carried ordnance. There are 10 wing "Hard points" and eight internal weapon points for missiles, bombs, torpedoes and depth charges. Germany operates eight of these aircraft, which are ex Dutch aircraft. They are in one squadron, which is based at NAS Nordholz. Orions, which are in service with other nations, are gradually being replaced by the Boeing "P-8 Poseidon". Whether Germany intends to do this also remains to be seen.

---

[41] Source https://commons.wikimedia.org/wiki/File:60-07_RIAT_Bthebest.JPG?uselang=en-gb

"Dornier Do228"

[42]"Do228 LM/NG"   no information

Role. Maritime patrol aircraft
Engines. 2 x Garrett AiResearch TPE-331-5-252D turboprops
Length. 16.54m   **Wingspan.** 16.97m   **Height.** 4.86m
Max Weight. 6,400 kgs   **Range.** 823 miles
Max Speed. 223 knots   **Service Ceiling.** 28,000 feet
Crew. 2

Notes
This aircraft first flew in 1981. It is operated by numerous civilian airlines around the world. Many of the worlds military have taken delivery of this aircraft as general transports and surveillance aircraft. The Germany Navy has two such aircraft for maritime surveillance and for pollution control. A third aircraft of an upgraded design is on order.

---

[42] Source http://commons.wikimedia.org/wiki/File:Dornier_228LT_Nordholz.jpg

45

Helicopters

"Westland Lynx"

[43]"Lynx"   US Navy/MCS Rachael L Leslie

Role. Anti-submarine & Search & Rescue
Engines. 2 x Rolls-Royce Gem turboshafts
Length. 15.24m   **Rotor Diameter.** 12.8m   **Height.** 3.76m
Max Weight. 11,750lbs   **Range.** 328 miles
Max Speed. 201 mph   **Service Ceiling.** 8,540 feet
Crew. 2-3
Armament. 2 x Torpedoes, 4 x Anti-ship missiles

Notes
The Lynx entered German Navy service in 1981, with the Mk88 variant. There are 21 currently in service. These will be replaced by the NH-90, in the near future.
The "Lynx" is a joint Anglo-French aircraft with Westland, (Britain), producing 70% of the aircraft and Aerospatiale, (France), producing the remaining 30%. It is without doubt one of the best helicopters in service anywhere in the world. To date, 13 nations still operate the Lynx.

---

[43] Source http://commons.wikimedia.org/wiki/File:German_marine_Lynx_departs_USS_Whidbey_Island.jpg

"Westland Sea King"

[44]"Sea King" Search & Rescue   user:Pajx

Role. Maritime Helicopter
Engines. 2 x Rolls-Royce Gnome turboshaft
Length. 17.02m   **Rotor diameter.** 18.9m   **Height.** 5.13m
Max Weight. 9,707 kgs   **Range.** 764 miles
Max Speed. 129 mph   **Service Ceiling.** 14,700 feet
Crew.4
Avionics. Dipping sonar, Sonobouy receiver, Magnetic Anomaly Detector and AKT-22 Data link.
Armament. 2 x Mk 46/66 anti-submarine torpedoes; Sonobuoys and flares; Nuclaer Depth charges.

Notes
These machines were built under license by Westland Helicopters. They differ greatly from the Sikorsky machines, with different engines and avionics. The German Navy uses these helicopters to supplement its fleet of "Lynx" helicopters and also in the Search & Rescue role. It entered service in Germany in 1969, with an order for twenty-two helicopters to replace the "Albatross" flying boat. It is expected that they will be replaced within this decade with the "NH-90" helicopter.

---

[44] Source http://commons.wikimedia.org/wiki/File:050625-Kiel-x06-600.jpg

"NH-90"

[45] "NH-90" of the Italian Navy   Julian Herzog

Role. Maritime Helicopter
Engines. 2 x General Electric T700/T6E1 turboshaft
Length. 19.56m   **Rotor diameter.** 16.3m   **Height.** 5.31m
Max Weight. 23,369lbs   **Range.** 559 miles
Max Speed. 186 mph   **Service Ceiling.** 19,686 feet
Crew. 3
Avionics. Forward looking Infra-Red (FLIR), Magnetic Anomaly Detector (MAD)
Armament. Anti-submarine torpedoes, Anti-ship missiles

Notes
This multi-national project helicopter first flew December 1995. France, Germany,
Italy and Holland were the original members with Portugal joining in 2001. Germany
has eighteen of these helicopters on order to replace its fleet of "Sea Kings" and
"Lynx" helicopters.

Drones

"Camcopter S-100"

[46]"S-100"

User:Stahlkocher

Role. Surveillance drone
Engine. 1 x Austro AE50R Wankel rotary engine
Length. 3.11m   **Rotor diameter.** 3.4m   **Height.** 1.12m
Max Weight. 441 lbs   **Range.** 112 miles
Max Speed. 138 mph   **Service Ceiling.** 18,000 feet
Crew. 0
Armament. 2 Hardpoints

Notes
The German Navy has chosen the S-100 as its primary unmanned surveillance system for shipboard operations, where it will be used for Surveillance and intelligence gathering. It has conducted successful trials aboard the "Braunschweig" class corvettes. Six drones have since been ordered.

Torpedoes

[47]"Black Shark"
Finmeccanica

The "Black Shark" heavyweight Torpedo is in service with the German Navy, plus 14 other navies. It is the very latest in technological advances. Its state of the art software will allow it to remain at the for-front of naval weaponry for the next 20 years. It is wire guided, fully stealth and self-homing. It is 6.3m long and 533mm in diameter. It can travel at 50 knots at range of 50 miles.

Lightweight Torpedo

[48]MU-90 torpedo
Causa83

Originally developed in the 1980's as a joint project between France and Italy, it wasn't until the 1990s that production began.
Weighting 304 kgs at a length of 2.85metres and a diameter of 323.7mm, this torpedo is capable of being fired from a ship or aircraft. It has a range of 5 to 12 miles depending on its speed of 50 knots maximum, with its pump-jet propulsion. The warhead is a shape charge weighting 32.7 kgs.

---

[47] Source http://www.finmeccanica.com/media/gallery-galleria/sistemi-difesa-defence-systems-photo?p_p_id=fnmrenderportlet_WAR_fnmpublishportlet_INSTANCE_tNK65bAIwEof&p_p_lifecycle=0&p_p_state=normal&p_p_mode=view&p_p_col_id=column-2&p_p_col_pos=1&p_p_col_count=2&_fnmrenderportlet_WAR_fnmpublishportlet_INSTANCE_tNK65bAIwEof_rend_0_offset=25
[48] Source http://commons.wikimedia.org/wiki/File:MU90_torpedo_01.jpg?uselang=en-gb

Missiles

[49]"IDAS missile"   Stahlkocher

This is the world's first surface-to-air missile for Submarines. It is of German origin, made for the Type 212 Submarine. It has a range of 20 miles and can engage low flying aircraft or Helicopters. Four missiles can be fitted into one torpedo tube and fired separately. The missile does not have a canister, it is fired clean from the tube.

[50]"Harpoon" anti-ship missile

US Navy/MCS Kevin V Cunningham

The "Harpoon" is one of the anti-ship missiles, used by the German Navy. It is a sea-skimming missile with a range of 124kms, at a speed of 537mph. The 488lb warhead is contact detonation. The ship launched and sub launched variants are 4.6 metres long, due to the extra rocket booster that is used for the initial launching. The air-launched variant is 3.8 metres long, as no rocket booster is needed for launching.

---

[49] Source http://commons.wikimedia.org/wiki/File:BGT_IDAS.jpg

[50] Source http://commons.wikimedia.org/wiki/File:Harpoon_missile_launch_aboard_USS_Shiloh.jpg

[51]"AM-39 Exocet"

David Monniaux

The Exocet is a surface-to-surface or air-to-surface anti-ship missile that made its name in the Falklands conflict between Britain and Argentina. In Argentine hands, the missile was used to great effect in sinking numerous British warships and auxiliaries and heavily damaging others. The missile is 4.7metres long, has a diameter of 348mm, with a speed just under Mach 1 and a range of 112 miles.

[52]"SeaRAM"

US Navy

This weapon system combines the radar of the "20mm Phalanx" and the missile capability of the "Rolling Airframe Missile" system. This system has an eleven-missile magazine, instead of 21. Each missile is 2.79 metres in length and has a range of nine kilometres, at a speed of mach 2. Whereas the RAM requires below deck support, the "SeaRAM", can be bolted to the deck of any vessel and operate independently. The new "Izumo" class of helicopter destroyers will be armed with this weapon.

---

[51] Source http://en.wikipedia.org/wiki/Exocet

[52] Source http://commons.wikimedia.org/wiki/File:SeaRAM_1.jpg

[53]"RIM-162" ESSM

The "RIM-162" is the Vertical Launch upgrade of the "RIM-7" missile. Because the missile is vertically launched, a larger more powerful engine is required. This also allows the missile to have an extended range of 50kms at a speed of mach 4. It is housed in the VLS "Mk 41" launcher. This is a four-missile canister, which can be deployed on smaller vessels, not just larger destroyers. The "Mk 48" launcher is a two-missile canister, for even smaller vessels

[54]"RIM-66" surface-to-air missile

This is the German Navy's primary long-range surface-to-air missile. It is 4.72 metres long and has a range of 40 to 167kms, depending if a "first stage" booster is fitted. The missile accelerates to a speed of mach 3.5, to a maximum service ceiling of 80,000 feet. It has both infra-red and semi-active terminal homing, to acquire its target. It was initially fired from surface mounted launchers, using bulky reloading systems. These have now been replaced by Vertical Launch Systems, which save weight and space.

---

[53] Source http://commons.wikimedia.org/wiki/File:RIM-162_ESSM_launched_from_USS_Carl_Vinson.jpg?uselang=en-gb
[54] Source http://commons.wikimedia.org/wiki/File:Sm2-Launch-USN.jpg

[55]"RAM" missile launcher
US Navy

This is an American developed short range missile system. It is has twenty-one missiles in a ready to fire container, which can be deployed on large or small surface warships. The missile is 2.79m long and has a range of approx five miles. It is currently deployed on the "Gepard" patrol boats and all of Germans larger surface warships.

[56]"Octuple Sea Sparrow"
US Navy/MCS Jordan R Beesley

The "RIM-7" is a short range, point defence missile system, which was introduced in 1976. The missile has a range of 19kms and a maximum speed of 2,645mph. The 90lb warhead can detonate on contact or do a proximity explosion. This has a kill radius of 27 feet. This system is still deployed on older units of the German Navy. Later upgraded "Sea Sparrow" missiles are deployed in Vertical Launch tubes.

[55] Source https://commons.wikimedia.org/wiki/File:RIM-116_RAM_Shot.jpg?uselang=en-gb
[56] Source http://commons.wikimedia.org/wiki/File:RIM-7_Sea_Sparrow_-_ID_070813-N-4166B-041.jpg

54

[57]"RBS-15"

Pibwl

This is a Swedish developed anti-ship missile, which is deployed on several units of the German fleet. It is 4.33m long and is 50cm in diameter. It carries a 200 kg warhead to a range of 250 kms. It is currently deployed on the "Braunschweig" class corvettes.

[58]"FIM-92 Stinger"

US Government

The Stinger missile is a shoulder held weapon, which was developed by the US Army to attack low flying aircraft. It is 1.52m long and has an effective range of three miles. It is currently used by the German navy on board several auxiliary vessels.

---

[57] Source http://commons.wikimedia.org/wiki/File:RBS15_missile.jpg?uselang=en-gb

[58] Source http://commons.wikimedia.org/wiki/File:StingerMissile.jpg

Guns

[59]"OtoMelara 76mm gun"
Mike

Developed by the Italian company Oto Melara, the 76mm Super Rapid has become somewhat of a standard when it comes to putting maximum firepower in a smaller calibre artillery piece. It is capable of fitting into most of the smaller type of naval vessels, such as patrol boats, corvettes and sloops. The rate of fire is impressive, with 120 rounds per minute. The gun's high rate of fire and availability of specialized ammunition make it well suited in varied roles such as short-range anti-missile point defence, anti-aircraft, anti-surface, and ground support. Specialized ammunition includes armour piercing, incendiary, directed fragmentation effects, and a guided round marketed as capable of destroying incoming missiles.

[60]"MLG27" autocannon
Rebell18190

This is a point-defence weapon, which can fire 1,700 rounds per minute at low flying aircraft or incoming, sea-skimming missiles. It was developed from the cannon, which is in the "Euro Fighter". It is fully automated and is fitted to almost every surface warship in the German Navy.

---

[59] Source http://commons.wikimedia.org/wiki/File:HMAS_Sydney_-03_(1702023083).jpg?uselang=en-gb
[60] Source http://commons.wikimedia.org/wiki/File:Autocannon_MLG27.jpg

[61]"12.7mm Machine Gun"
This powerful Machine Gun is used by almost every nation in the world. It combines high fire rate (1,200 rounds per minute), long range, accuracy and sheer stopping power. It is used on most smaller warships. It is also used in some Maritime patrol Helicopters.

[62]"40mm Bofors"

This weapon was first built just before World War 2. With a range of 12.500metres and a fire rate of 330 rounds per minute, it is used by almost all of the world's armed forces. The German navy still use it aboard their older vessels.

[61] Source http://en.wikipedia.org/wiki/M2_Browning#mediaviewer/File:Machine_gun_M2_1.jpg
[62] Source http://commons.wikimedia.org/wiki/File:HMAS-Castlemaine-gun-3-1.jpg?uselang=en-gb

THE MODERN DUTCH NAVY

INTRODUCTION

The Dutch Navy has always been one of the most powerful in Europe. Dating back to the 1600's, it was always a match for the Royal Navy, Spanish Navy and the French Navy. Holland also had its own colonies, mainly in the East Indies, (now Indonesia). In the Second World War, the Dutch Navy, even with Holland occupied, performed brilliantly against the Japanese in the Pacific. Out-battling the Americans and the British against the Japanese.

After the war, Holland, like all the other colonial powers, had to accept the fact the loss of its colonies and adjust itself accordingly. The navy was now concentrating on fighting the Cold War against the Warsaw Pact. All of its ships and aircraft were designed to operate in the North Sea and the Atlantic Ocean as part of the NATO Alliance. Most Dutch vessels were assigned to the "Standing Naval Force Atlantic", whose primary job was to safeguard the seaways across the Atlantic to reinforce Europe from the US.

During this period, the Dutch navy was at least twice the size that it is now. However, since the end of the Cold War the "peace dividend" affected the Dutch Navy the same as every other western fleet. Many vessels have been decommissioned or sold without any replacement vessel being built.

Few would argue that the Dutch have some very fine and capable warships. The "Walrus" class of submarine's are some of the most powerful diesel-electric boats in the world and are thought of very highly in NATO circles. These boats are going through a midlife modernisation program now to enable them to operate well into the next decade.

The "Karel Doorman" class frigates are nearing the end of their service lives, with only two of the original eight still in Dutch service, the rest transferred to other navies. Soon this will only leave the four ships of the "De Zeven Provincien" class to be the "teeth" of the surface fleet. These frigates will have to be available to NATO in the Atlantic and to coalition operations on the War on Terror and against Somali pirates in the Indian Ocean. Leaser vessels, such as the "Holland" class patrol will undoubtedly be called on to fill the gaps on long-range deployments.

The amphibious assault ships of the "Rotterdam" and "Johan de Witt" class are very capable ships and have proven themselves in combat operations and humanitarian relief around the Indian Ocean. The new "Karel Doorman" class replenishment/ combat support ship, will ease the pressure on the surface fleet, with her being capable of many tasks in support of operations.

The last six of the "Tripartite" mine sweepers are coming to the end of their service lives and there hasn't been any word on whether these vessels will be replaced or just decommissioned. The Dutch do need some kind of anti-mine capability as most of the sea lanes, in and out of Dutch ports are in between old mine fields left over from the war.

The "Lynx" helicopter is being replaced by the "NH-90", which is a larger and more capable machine, which will help bring Dutch anti-submarine capability to a very modern standard.

The Dutch are going to have to ask themselves some very hard questions soon. With current commitments, the Dutch fleet is very stretched indeed. The War on Terror and anti-piracy operations will be on going well into the next decade, plus now there is the problem of Russia beginning to flex its muscle again. Not only on its land borders with old satellite states but, the Russian Navy is also starting to grow in confidence once more. The Russian fleet, even though much of it isn't very modern, is still very large and very threatening. Dutch naval spending will have to increase just to keep pace of this, once again, very uncertain world.

63

"Naval Jack"

63 Source http://commons.wikimedia.org/wiki/File:Naval_Jack_of_the_Netherlands.svg

Pennant Numbers

Ship	Pennant Number	Ship	Pennant Number
Submarines		**Mine Sweepers**	
Walrus	S802	Makkum	M857
Zeeleeuw	S803	Schiedam	M860
Dolfijn	S808	Urk	M861
Bruinvis	S810	Zierikzee	M862
		Vlaardingen	M863
Amphibious Assault Ships		Willemstad	M864
Rotterdam	L800	**Replenishment Ship**	
Johan de Witt	L801	Karel Doorman	A833
Frigates		**Diving Support Ships**	
De Zeven Provincien	F802	Cerberus	A851
Tromp	F803	Argus	A852
De Ruyter	F804	Nautilus	A853
Evertsen	F805	Hydra	A854
Van Speijk	F828		
Van Amstel	F831	**Survey Ships**	
		Snellius	A802
Patrol Boats		Luymes	A803
Holland	P840		
Zeeland	P841	**Submarine Support**	
Friesland	P842	Mercuur	A900
Groningen	P843		
		Tugboats	
Logistic Support Ship		Linge	A874
Pelikaan	A804	Regge	A875
		Hunze	A876
Training Ships		Rotte	A877
Van Kinsbergen	A902	Gouwe	A878
Urania	Y8050	Breezand	Y8018
		Balgzand	Y8019
Landing Craft		Scheldt	Y8055
LCU	L9525	Wierbalg	Y8056
	L9526	Malzwin	Y8057
	L9527	Zuidwal	Y8058
	L9528	Westwal	Y8059
	L9529		
		Cutters	
		Jaguar	P810
		Panther	P811
		Puma	P812

60

Submarines

"Walrus" class

[64]"Walrus"   US Navy/MCS Marlowe P Dix

Name	Pennant	Completed	Builder
Walrus	S802	1992	RDM
Zeeleeuw	S803	1990	RDM
Dolfijn	S808	1993	RDM
Bruinvis	S810	1994	RDM

Displacement. 2,800 tonnes   **Dimensions.** 67.7m x 8.4m x 7.5m
Speed. 21 knots   **Complement.** 33
Armament. 6 x 533mm torpedo tubes plus 12 reloads

Notes
These four boats are the replacements for the previous trio of the "Zwardvis" class.
These diesel-electric boats brought the Dutch submarine fleet up to date with modern
requirements for underwater warfare.
The lead boat, "Walrus", was badly damaged by an electrical fire during construction
and was commissioned after the second boat, "Zeeleeuw" in 1992. These boats are
some of the most advanced in the world. They were one of the first class of boats to
be constructed with the "X" shape of planes at the stern, which enables them to
operate in shallow waters. This makes them ideal for intelligence gathering near an

---

[64] Source http://commons.wikimedia.org/wiki/File:081028-N-6011D-013.jpg?uselang=en-gb

enemy coast. Their performance in NATO exercises have been impressive, with "Walrus" in 1999 penetrating a US carrier battle group and sinking the "USS Theodore Roosevelt" and several escorts before escaping. They have also seen action in the Indian Ocean, participating in operations in Afghanistan and other international and coalition missions.

In 2008, it was announced that these boats would undergo a midlife modernisation program to enable them to operate until at least 2025. "Walrus" will be the last to undergo the modernisation and should return to active service in 2019.

[65]"Walrus"   Aubrey Dale

[65] Source http://commons.wikimedia.org/wiki/File:HNLMS_Walrus_(S802)_in_2008.jpg?uselang=en-gb

Amphibious Assault Ships

"Rotterdam" class

[66]"Rotterdam"

US Navy/MCS Jared King

Name	Pennant	Completed	Builder
Rotterdam	L800	1998	Schelde Naval Shipbuilding

Displacement. 12,750 tonnes   **Dimensions.** 166m x 25m x 5.8m
Speed. 19 knots   **Complement.** 128
Armament. 2 x 30mm Goalkeeper CIWS; 4 x 20mm Oerlikon
Landing Craft. 6 x LCU or 4 x LCVP

Notes
The "Rotterdam" is the result of an international project between Spain and Holland for common ship design to operate inside NATO. Two Dutch ships have so far been completed and two Spanish ships. The British also completed four ships, which are based on this design, however, they are not of this class. The two Spanish ships are identical to each other, but the two Dutch ships are often referred to as separate classes. Germany did plan to build ships of its own but these have not been ordered due to budget cuts.
This ship is able to embark and put ashore a maximum of seven hundred and fifty troops and equipment using its landing craft or helicopters. Up to six helicopters can

be embarked using the very large stern helicopter deck and the hangar. The helicopters not normally carried. Up to ninety light armoured vehicles can be carried or thirty-two main battle tanks.

This vessel is also well suited to provide humanitarian assistance. There is a well-equipped hospital on board with an operating theatre and an intensive care ward. There is a desalination plant on board to convert seawater in drinking water.

A second vessel was built in 2007, "Johan de Witt", to a larger design, which is normally referred to as a separate class.

[67]"Rotterdam"   Koninklijke Marine

"Johan de Witt" class

[68]"Johan de Witt"   Joost J Bakker

Name	Pennant	Completed	Builder
Johan de Witt	L801	2007	Schelde Naval Shipbuilding

Displacement. 16,800 tonnes   **Dimensions.** 176m x 29m x 6m
Speed. 19 knots   **Complement.** 146
Armament. 2 x 30mm Goalkeeper CIWS; 4-6 12.7mm Machine guns
Landing Craft. 4 x LCVP; 2 x LCU; 2 x LCAC

Notes
This ship is the result of the international Dutch and Spanish program, known as the "Enforcer" program. She is the second ship from the Dutch side of the program. She was commissioned nine years after the "Rotterdam" and is considerably bigger. The superstructure is one deck higher to accommodate extra command and control facilities. Her troop carrying capacity is roughly the same as "Rotterdam", but she able to carry up to one hundred and seventy light armoured vehicles or thirty-three main battle tanks. The larger flight deck and hangar can accommodate six heavy lift helicopters and the larger stern docking well is big enough to take two LCAC's. As with the "Rotterdam", this vessel is well suited to provide humanitarian assistance. There is a well-equipped hospital on board with an operating theatre and an intensive

[68] Source http://commons.wikimedia.org/wiki/File:HNLMS_Johan_de_Witt_(L801)_(1).jpg

care ward. There is a desalination plant on board to convert seawater in drinking water.

The "Johan de Witt", has spent a considerable amount of time operating East of Suez in support of international and coalition operations. Much of that has been off the Horn of Africa disrupting Somali pirate activities. She has been very successful in this role and sometimes acts as a flagship for coordinated actions. She has also helped out ashore with humanitarian efforts in Somalia, providing drinking water and medical assistance.

[69]"Johan de Witt"   Gerben van Es/Ministerie van Defensie

---

[69] Source http://commons.wikimedia.org/wiki/File:HNLMS_Johan_de_Witt_(L801)_with_LCVPs.jpg?uselang=en-gb

Landing Craft

"LCU Mk2"

[70]"LCU Mk2"

Ikjanus

Name	Pennant	Completed	Builder
	L9525	1998	
	L9526	1999	
	L9527	1999	
	L9528	1998	
	L9529	1999	

Displacement. 255 tonnes　　　**Dimensions.** 36.3m x 6.85m x 1.4m
Speed. 9 knots　　　**Complement.** 7
Armament. 2 x 12.7mm Machine guns

Notes

These landing craft were built to operate from the "Rotterdam" and "Johan de Witt" assault ships. These vessels were upgraded to be able to carry more equipment. They can carry up to 130 marines or sixty-five tonnes of equipment or one main battle tank.

---

[70] Source https://commons.wikimedia.org/wiki/File:NL_LCU_MK2.jpg?uselang=en-gb

"LCVP Mk 5"

71"Mk 5"   Sean Clee

Displacement. 24 tonnes   **Dimensions.** 15.7m x 4.27m x 0.65m
Speed. 25 knots   **Complement.** 3

Notes
These landing craft were built to operate from the "Rotterdam" and "Johan de Witt"
assault ships. These have replaced the "Mk 2" and "Mk 3" landing craft. The Dutch
Marines operate twelve of these landing craft. They have been built by Vosper
Thorneycroft of the UK and are capable of carrying 38 troops or eight tonnes of
equipment.

---

71 Source http://commons.wikimedia.org/wiki/File:A_Royal_Marine_LCVP_Landing_Craft_MOD_45150169.jpg

Frigates

"Karel Doorman" class

72"Van Amstel"   US Navy/Jeremy L Grisham

Name	Pennant	Completed	Builder
Van Amstel	F831	1993	Schelde Naval Shipbuilding
Van Speijk	F828	1995	Schelde Naval Shipbuilding

Displacement. 2,800 tonnes   **Dimensions.** 122.3m x 14.4m x 6.1m
Speed. 30 knots   **Complement.** 154
Armament. 1 x 76mm Oto Melara 2 x 30mm Goalkeeper CIWS;
       2-6 7.62mm Machine guns; 16 VLS Sea Sparrow SAM
       8 x Harpoon; 2 x twin torpedo tubes
Aircraft. 1 x ASW Helicopter

Notes
These two frigates are all that is left of the original eight ships of the "Karel Doorman" class. "Karel Doorman F827" and "Willem van der Zaan F829" were decommissioned in 2005 and were transferred to Belgium. "Tjerk Hiddes F830" and "Abraham van der Hulst F832" were decommissioned in 2004 and were transferred to Chile. "Van Nes F833" and "Van Galen F834" were decommissioned in 2006 and were transferred to Portugal.

---

72 Source http://commons.wikimedia.org/wiki/File:HMS_Van_Amstel_F831_USN-8154G-232_cropped.jpg

Many commentators consider these vessels as scaled down versions of the
"Kortenaers" class. When these ships were built, they were regarded as one of the
most powerful frigates in the world. Their well-balanced weapon suite enabled them
to deal with any surface or sub-surface threat and any airborne threat. They were
one of the first class of vessels to be fitted with Vertical Launch tubes for Surface-to-
Air missiles. The installation of these missiles is unique, as the VLS tubes are along
side the helicopter hangar.
The Dutch and Belgian vessels have been modernized, with new Radars and
Sensor's, and the helicopter hangar has been rebuilt to accommodate the larger "NH-
90" type helicopter.
Due to budget restrictions, it is unclear whether the two last remaining ships of this
class will refitted to continue in service or be decommissioned and offered abroad.

[73]"Van Speijk"   Koninklijke Marine

[73] Source http://commons.wikimedia.org/wiki/File:Hr._Ms._Van_Speijk_(F828).jpg

"De Zeven Provincien" class

74"Tromp"   Koninklijke Marine

Name	Pennant	Completed	Builder
De Zeven Provincien	F802	2002	Royal Schelde
Tromp	F803	2003	Royal Schelde
De Ruyter	F804	2004	Royal Schelde
Evertsen	F805	2005	Royal Schelde

Displacement. 6,050 tonnes   **Dimensions.** 144.24m x 18.8m x 5.18m
Speed. 30 knots   **Complement.** 174
Armament. 1 x 127mm Oto Melara gun; 2 x 30mm Goalkeeper CIWS;
     4-6 x 7.62mm Machine guns; 4 x 12.7mm Machine guns
     40 cell VLS SAM
     8 x Harpoon; 2 x twin torpedo tubes
Aircraft. 1 x ASW Helicopter

Notes
This class of very modern frigates are the replacements for the "Tromp" and "Jacob van Heesmarck" classes.

---

74 Source http://commons.wikimedia.org/wiki/File:Hr._Ms._Tromp_(F803).jpg

These vessels represent the latest in Dutch ship design and technology. The weapon suite is balanced to deal with surface, sub-surface and airborne threats. The Vertical Launch System comprises of a forty-cell magazine. Thirty-two cells house the long-range "Standard SM-2" missile, while the remaining eight cells house quadruple "Evolved Sea Sparrow" missiles. It is possible that these vessels will be given an anti-ballistic missile capability in the near future. "Tromp" has conducted tests in the Pacific to see if this upgrade is feasible.

Stealth features have been built into the design, giving the ships a very clean look with no protruding features. It is hard to see the eight "Harpoon" missiles and the anti-submarine torpedo tubes. The anti-submarine helicopter has been upgraded from the "Westland Lynx" to the "NH-90".

Since completion, these vessels have been very busy conducting operations not only in the North Sea and Atlantic Ocean, but also in the Mediterranean Sea and in the Indian Ocean. Anti-piracy patrols off Somalia have been very successful and very time consuming. They have also taken part in coalition operations in the Arabian Sea. There were plans to fit these vessels with "Tomahawk" cruise missiles, but this has been put on hold for the time being.

[75]"De Zeven Provincien"   Ministerie van Defensie

Patrol Ships

"Holland" class

[76]"Holland"

Ministerie van Defensie

Name	Pennant	Completed	Builder
Holland	P840	2012	Damen Schelde
Zeeland	P841	2013	Damen Schelde
Friesland	P842	2013	Damen Schelde
Groningen	P843	2013	Damen Schelde

Displacement. 3,750 tonnes   **Dimensions.** 108.4m x 16m x 4.55m
Speed. 21.5 knots   **Complement.** 54
Armament. 1 x 76mm Oto Melara gun; 1 x 30mm Oto Melara Marlin
       6 x 7.62mm Machine guns; 2 x 12.7mm Oto Melara Hitrole
Aircraft. 1 x ASW Helicopter

Notes
These four offshore patrol vessels were designed to operate around the world, not just in the North Sea, to deal with small leaser threats, such as smuggling and anti-piracy duties. They were funded for by the sale of older Dutch Navy vessels to other countries.
The hull has been constructed of thicker steel for added protection giving them in very heavy displacement. The weapon suite is designed around the "small surface action" theory. It comprises mainly of quick firing Oto Melara type weapons. These can also be used in the anti-aircraft or anti-missile role. There is a very large

[76] Source http://commons.wikimedia.org/wiki/File:HNLMS_Holland.jpg?uselang=en-gb

helicopter deck to the stern and a hangar and support facilities to operate an "NH-90" type, medium helicopter. This isn't primarily for anti-submarine search, but for search & seizure duties. A fast rescue boat and two fast special force's boats are carried along with, maybe, an extra forty personnel if needed. These are primarily for patrols off the Horn of Africa dealing with pirates. Their range of five thousand miles makes them ideal for these kinds of deployments.

[77]"Zeeland"   Mark Harkin

[77] Source http://commons.wikimedia.org/wiki/File:P841_Zeeland.jpg?uselang=en-gb

Minesweepers

"Tripartite" class

[78]"Urk"

Mark Harkin

Name	Pennant	Completed	Builder
Makkum	M857	1985	Van der Giessen
Schiedam	M860	1986	Van der Giessen
Urk	M861	1986	Van der Giessen
Zierikzee	M862	1987	Van der Giessen
Vlaardingen	M863	1988	Van der Giessen
Willemstad	M864	1989	Van der Giessen

Displacement. 543 tonnes   **Dimensions.** 51.5m x 8.9m x 3.8m
Speed. 15 knots   **Complement.** 44
Armament. 1 x 20mm gun

Notes
The "Alkmaar" class of minesweepers are the Dutch ships of the very successful "Tripartite" program. This international program consisted of France, Holland and Belgium. France and Holland built fifteen vessels each, while Belgium built ten. However, with decommissions, transfers and export sales, there are now seven countries benefiting from the program. Holland constructed the propulsion systems, Belgium the electronics and France the mine hunting equipment.
There are only six vessels still in Dutch service, the rest have been decommissioned or transferred to other navies. "Alkmaar M850", "Delfzijl M851", "Dordrecht M852",

[78] Source http://commons.wikimedia.org/wiki/File:M861_HNLMS_Urk_(8644186262).jpg?uselang=en-gb

"Harlingen M854" and "Scheveningen M855" have all been decommissioned and transferred to Latvia. "Haarlem M853", "Maasluis M856", "Middelburg M858" and "Hellevoetsluis M859" and all been decommissioned and laid up.
The Dutch ships have been constantly upgraded to function in a modern environment, but it is unclear how long it will be until the final six ships are decommissioned and replaced.

[79]"Urk"

Mark Harkin

[79] Source https://commons.wikimedia.org/wiki/File:M861_HNLMS_Urk_(8643089511).jpg?uselang=en-gb

Replenishment/Support Ship

"Karel Doorman" class

[80]"Karel Doorman"

kees torn

Name	Pennant	Completed	Builder
Karel Doorman	A833	2015	Damen Schelde

Displacement. 27,800 tonnes   **Dimensions.** 204.7m x 30.4m x 7.8m
Speed. 18 knots   **Complement.** 150
Armament. 2 x 30mm Goalkeeper CIWS; 2 x 30mm Oto Melara Marlin
           4 x 12.7mm Oto Melara Hitrole; 6-8 x 7.62 Machine guns
Landing Craft. 2 x LCVP; 2 x RHIB

Notes
This vessel is the replacement for the "Zuiderkruis", which was scrapped in 2014 and for the "Amsterdam", which was decommissioned and sold to Peru in the same year. It was announced that the "Karel Doorman" would not enter service due to budget cuts but this has since been reversed.
She is able to operate in the replenishment role or the amphibious assault role. She is able to carry and transfer at sea diesel fuel, aviation fuel, fresh water, ammunition and dry stores. In the amphibious role, the ship can accommodate three hundred personnel in total. Most of these are to support the helicopter support, which can be embarked and supported in the very large hangar and flight deck at the stern. Up to six medium or two "Chinoocks" can be embarked. Two "LCVP" landing craft and two "RHIB" fast boats are permanently embarked.

The weapon suite is the same as the "Holland" class patrol boats. They are mainly Oto Melara point defence guns, plus also smaller calibre weapons. It is thought that these may have been added with future patrols off Somalia in mind.

Even before she has been commissioned, she has been very busy. Just after she had completed her sea trials in 2014, "Karel Doorman" was sent to West Africa with stores and medical supplies to aid in the international fight against the Ebola outbreak.

[81]"Karel Doorman"   Ministerie van Defensie

[81] Source https://commons.wikimedia.org/wiki/File:JSS_Karel_Doorman_in_Den_Helder.jpg?uselang=en-gb

Diving Support Ships

"Cerberus" class

[82]"Nautilus"

Quistnix

Name	Pennant	Completed	Builder
Cerberus	A851	1992	Damen Daman
Argus	A852	1992	Damen Daman
Nautilus	A853	1992	Damen Daman
Hrdra	A854	1992	Damen Daman

Displacement. 223 tonnes
Speed. 10 knots

Dimensions. 27.3m x 8.5m x 1.5m
Complement. 6

Notes

These four vessels are the replacements for the "Triton" class. These vessels are larger and more capable. They are not often seen at sea because of their flat-bottomed hulls. They mainly operate close to shore or in river ways.

There is a double decompression chamber and a diving bell on board to aid in diving operations.

In 1997, "Hydra" was extended by 10.5 metres, her displacement went up to 297 tonnes and her speed was increased to 13 knots. This gave her the ability to embark twenty-two divers and additional crew accommodation improvements, such as a new galley, a laundry room and a day room for the increased crew of nine. In 2008, "Nautilus" was extended by the same amount, but her speed remains at 10 knots.

---

[82] Source http://commons.wikimedia.org/wiki/File:Rotterdam_Havendagen_2009_-_A853_Hr_Ms_Nautilus.jpg

Survey Ships

"Snellius" class

[83]"Snellius"   Vermerris

Name	Pennant	Completed	Builder
Snellius	A802	2003	Damen/Schelde
Luymes	A803	2004	Damen/Schelde

Displacement. 1,875 tonnes   **Dimensions.** 81.42m x 13.1m x 4m
Speed. 12.5 knots   **Complement.** 18

Notes
These two vessels are hydrographic survey ships. They are used to map and survey the seabed. They also carry out general patrols along Holland's coast and participate in fishery protection duties. A limited anti-pollution capability is also embarked. These ships were the first Dutch ships to be built in Romania and Holland. Crew accommodation is very good and has set a new standard for habitability.

---

[83] Source http://upload.wikimedia.org/wikipedia/commons/7/7e/Hr.Ms._Snellius.jpg?uselang=en-gb

Submarine Support Ship"

"Mercuur" class

[84]"Mercuur"

Josh Bennett

Name	Pennant	Completed	Builder
Mercuur	A900	1987	Damen Schelde

Displacement. 1,500 tonnes
Speed. 14 knots

Dimensions. 64.8m x 12m x 4.33m
Complement. 27

Notes

The "Mercuur" is a support vessel for submarine operations. She is mainly used for testing weapon systems and general patrol duties. She can fire and retrieve torpedoes for testing and evaluation. She is fitted to carry two 20mm guns, but these are not embarked in peacetime.

---

[84] Source
https://commons.wikimedia.org/wiki/File:The_Royal_Netherlands_Navy_submarine_support_ship_HNLMS_Mercuur_(A900)_co
nducts_maritime_operations_June_15,_2013,_in_the_Baltic_Sea_during_Baltic_Operations_(BALTOPS)_2013_130615-N-
ZL691-228.jpg?uselang=en-gb

Logistic Support Ship

"Pelikaan" class

[85]"Pelikaan"

Ministerie van Defensie

Name	Pennant	Completed	Builder
Pelikaan	A804	2006	Damen Schelde

Displacement. 1,150 tonnes   **Dimensions.** 65.4m x 13.2m x 3m
Speed. 14.5 knots   **Complement.** 13
Armament. 2 x 12.7mm Machine guns

Notes
This vessel is multi-purpose ship designed for work in the West Indies. She carries military equipment and personnel between islands and generally keeps a watch on activities. She is also capable of providing humanitarian relief.

---

[85] Source http://commons.wikimedia.org/wiki/File:HNLMS_Pelikaan.jpg?uselang=en-gb

82

Navy Cutters

"Jaguar" class

[86]"Jaguar" Mindef

Name	Pennant	Completed	Builder
Jaguar	P810	1998	Damen
Panther	P811	1999	Damen
Puma	P812	1999	Damen

Displacement. 195 tonnes **Dimensions.** 42.8m x 6.7m x 2.5m
Speed. 27 knots **Complement.** 11
Armament. 1 x 12.7mm Machine gun

Notes
These cutters are part of the Caribbean patrol. Officially, they belong to the navy, but
they are in fact operated by the Coast Guard. Their duties include general policing,
anti-piracy, anti-drug trafficking and search and rescue.

---

[86] Source http://commons.wikimedia.org/wiki/File:Stan_Patrol_P810_Jaguar_Dutch_Caribbean_Coastguard.jpg?uselang=en-gb

Training Ships

"Urania" class

[87]"Urania"

Koninklijke Marine

Name	Pennant	Completed	Builder
Urania	Y8050	1928	Haarlemsche Scheepsbouwmaatschappij

Displacement. 75 tonnes
Speed. 16.5 knots

Dimensions. 26.85m x 6.04m x 3m
Complement. 17

Notes

This yacht was originally named "Tromp". She acquired by navy in 1938 and then captured and used by the Germans in World War 2. In 1946, she was returned to Holland where she has been used as a training vessel ever since. In 2001-2004, she was given a complete modernisation and continues as before.

"Van Kinsbergen" class

[88]"Van Kinsbergen"   E Vroom

Name	Pennant	Completed	Builder
Van Kinsbergen	A902	1999	Damen

Displacement. 630 tonnes   **Dimensions.** 41.5m x 9.2m x 3.3m
Speed. 12.8 knots   **Complement.** 24

Notes
This training vessel was specifically built for the task. She is designed to train practical seamanship and navigation. She is crewed by a mix of civilian and military personnel. The senior officers are military. She is equipped with a crane and a rigid boat.

---

[88] Source http://www.shipspotting.com/gallery/photo.php?lid=1379345

Tugboats

"Linge" class

[89]"Rotte"   Quistnix

Name	Pennant	Completed	Builder
Linge	A874	1987	Delta, Sliedrecht
Regge	A875	1987	Delta, Sliedrecht
Hunze	A876	1987	Delta, Sliedrecht
Rotte	A877	1987	Delta, Sliedrecht
Gouwe	A878	1997	Delta, Sliedrecht

Displacement. 200 tonnes   **Dimensions.** 27.45m x 8.3m x 2.7m
Speed. 12 knots   **Complement.** 5

Notes
These large tugboats can be seen at Holland's major ports conducting basic harbour duties. They are capable of ocean work if necessary. "Gouwe" was ordered later on and is built to a slightly higher specification.

"Breezand" class

[90]"Breezand"

Piet van der Veer

Name	Pennant	Completed	Builder
Breezand	Y8018	1989	Delta, Sliedrecht
Balgzand	Y8019	1990	Delta, Sliedrecht

Displacement. 58 tonnes

Dimensions. 16.5m x 5.3m x 1.8m

Speed. 10 knots

Complement. 5

Notes
This small class of harbour tugboats can be seen at the naval ports of Holland, performing basic harbour duties.

---

[90] Source http://www.shipspotting.com/gallery/photo.php?lid=2073179

"Scheldt" class

[91]"Zuidwal"   William Hill

Name	Pennant	Completed	Builder
Scheldt	Y8055	1987	Delta, Sliedrecht
Wierbalg	Y8056	1987	Delta, Sliedrecht
Malzwin	Y8057	1986	Delta, Sliedrecht
Zuidwal	Y8058	1986	Delta, Sliedrecht
Westwal	Y8059	1986	Delta, Sliedrecht

Displacement. 23 tonnes   **Dimensions.** 10.8m x 3.76m x 1.6m
Speed. 9 knots   **Complement.** 2

Notes
These very small tugboats perform basic harbour duties at some of the smaller ports
of Holland.

Naval Aviation

"NH-90" helicopter

[92]"NH-90"

Gerard van der Schaaf

Role. Maritime Helicopter
Engines. 2 x General Electric T700/T6E1 turbo shaft
Length. 19.56m   **Rotor diameter.** 16.3m   **Height.** 5.31m
Max Weight. 23,369lbs   **Range.** 559 miles
Max Speed. 186 mph   **Service Ceiling.** 19,686 feet
Crew. 3
Avionics. Forward looking Infra-Red (FLIR), Magnetic Anomaly Detector (MAD)
Armament. Anti-submarine torpedoes, Anti-ship missiles

Notes
This multi-national project helicopter first flew December 1995. France, Germany, Italy and Holland were the original members with Portugal joining in 2001. The Dutch Navy operates twenty of these helicopters, replacing the "Westland Lynx".

"Westland Lynx"

[93]"Lynx"   Rob Schleiffert

Role. Anti-submarine & Search & Rescue
Engines. 2 x Rolls-Royce Gem turbo shafts

Length. 15.24m	**Rotor Diameter.** 12.8m	**Height.** 3.76m
Max Weight. 11,750lbs	**Range.** 328 miles	
Max Speed. 201 mph	**Service Ceiling.** 8,540 feet	

Crew. 2-3
Armament. 2 x Torpedoes, 4 x Anti-ship missiles

Notes
The Lynx entered French Navy service in 1979, with 20 currently in service.
It is a joint Anglo-French aircraft with Westland, (Britain), producing 70% of the
aircraft and Aerospatiale, (France), producing the remaining 30%. It is without doubt
one of the best helicopters in service anywhere in the world. To date, 13 nations still
operate the Lynx. In 2006, the Lynx Wildcat began to be developed. Dutch "Lynx's"
are to be replaced by the "NH-90".

---

[93] Source http://commons.wikimedia.org/wiki/File:Lynx_(12757425025).jpg?uselang=en-gb

Guns

[94]127/54 Otobreda Compact gun

US Navy/Jeffrey W Loshaw

This dual-purpose artillery weapon can fire various types of ammunition. It is a 5-inch gun with a ready-to-fire magazine of 66 rounds. It can fire 40 rounds per minute, to a range of 30 kms. The gun barrel is water-cooled. This weapon is gradually being replaced by the 127/64, in newer vessels.

[95]"12,7mm Browning Machine Gun"

US Navy/Robert R McRill

This powerful Machine Gun is used by almost every nation in the world. It combines high fire rate (1,200 rounds per minute), long range, accuracy and sheer stopping power. It is used on most smaller warships. More are being deployed on larger warships to counter pirate attacks. It is also used in some Maritime patrol Helicopters.

---

[94] Source http://commons.wikimedia.org/wiki/File:Otobreda_127.54_Compact_on_ARV_Mariscal_Sucre_(F-21)_-_1987.jpg
[95] Source http://en.wikipedia.org/wiki/M2_Browning_machine_gun

[96]"7.62mm Machine gun"

US Navy/Johansen Laurel

This machine gun is used by almost all of the armed forces in the world. As a general-purpose machine gun, it can be used and deployed anywhere. It is mainly deployed on smaller craft and patrol boats of the Dutch Navy. It is now being deployed on larger vessels to counter pirate attacks.

[97]"Goalkeeper CIWS"

Amanda Reynolds

This is a seven-barrelled automated weapon, which can be deployed on almost every type of surface vessel. It can fire 4,200 30mm rounds per minute, out to a maximum effective range of 2000 metres. It was developed in Holland and is used by many of the world's navies. Compared to the 20mm Phalanx, this weapon is not just bolted to the deck; it does have workings below deck, which does make this weapon more cumbersome.

---

[96] Source http://commons.wikimedia.org/wiki/File:US_Navy_040714-N-8977L-012_Master-at-Arms_3rd_Class_Rick_Bolander_of_Marquette,_Mich.,_mans_a_7.62mm_M-60_machine_gun_aboard_the_patrol_catamaran_Defender_One.jpg?uselang=en-gb

[97] Source http://commons.wikimedia.org/wiki/File:Goalkeeper_CIWS_Gun_Opens_Fire_During_Exercise_at_Sea_MOD_45151583.jpg

[98]"Otobreda 76mm Gun"
User:Ketil

Developed by the Italian company Oto Melara, the 76mm Super Rapid has become somewhat of a standard when it comes to putting maximum firepower in a smaller calibre artillery piece. It is capable of fitting into most of the smaller type of naval vessels, such as patrol boats, corvettes and sloops. The rate of fire is impressive, with 120 rounds per minute. The gun's high rate of fire and availability of specialized ammunition make it well suited in varied roles such as short-range anti-missile point defence, anti-aircraft, anti-surface, and ground support. Specialized ammunition includes armour piercing, incendiary, directed fragmentation effects, and a guided round marketed as capable of destroying incoming missiles.

[99]"30mm Oto Melara Marlin"
Oto Melara

This is a 30mm weapon, which can be deployed on surface warships of almost any size. It can fire 800 rounds per minute out to an effective range of three kilometres. It can engage surface and airborne targets. It is a relatively new weapon, which is just beginning to make its mark.

---

[98] Source http://en.wikipedia.org/wiki/Otobreda_76_mm#mediaviewer/File:Nansen-oto75mm-2006-07-03.jpg

[99] Source http://www.otomelara.it/products-services/naval-systems/marlin-ws

[100]"12.7mm Hitrole"

Oto Melara

This weapon is just beginning to come into naval circles, with it being deployed on the very latest warships. It is operated by a single person, which is at a separate console in a protected position. It can be used against in coming aircraft or sea-skimming missiles. Anti-surface targets are also within its capability.

[101]"Oerlikon 20mm cannon"   Chase me ladies, I'm the Cavalry

This weapon is an earlier version of the "KBA 25/80mm" gun. It is a manually operated weapon, with aiming being done through an optical sight. It can fire 450 rounds per minute, to a range of over a thousand yards.

---

[100] Source http://www.otomelara.it/products-services/naval-systems/hitrole-n
[101] Source http://commons.wikimedia.org/wiki/File:20mm_gun.jpg

Missiles

[102]"RIM-7 Sea Sparrow"
US Navy/MCS Jordan R Beesley

The "RIM-7" is a short range, point defence missile system, which was introduced in 1976. The missile has a range of 19kms and a maximum speed of 2,645mph. The 90lb warhead can detonate on contact or do a proximity explosion. This has a kill radius of 27 feet. Most of these launchers are deployed on earlier or smaller units of the Dutch Navy. Later upgraded "Sea Sparrow" missiles are deployed in Vertical Launch tubes.

[103]"RIM-162" ESSM
US Navy/MCS Matthew J Haran

The "RIM-162" is the Vertical Launch upgrade of the "RIM-7" missile. A larger more powerful engine is required because the missile is vertically launched. This also allows the missile to have an extended range of 50kms at a speed of mach 4. It is housed in the VLS "Mk 41" launcher. This is a four-missile canister, which can be deployed on smaller vessels, not just larger destroyers. The "Mk 48" launcher is a two-missile canister, for even smaller vessels.

---

[102] Source http://commons.wikimedia.org/wiki/File:RIM_7_fire.jpg

[103] Source http://commons.wikimedia.org/wiki/File:RIM-162_ESSM_launched_from_USS_Carl_Vinson.jpg?uselang=en-gb

[104]"Harpoon" missile

US Navy

The "Harpoon" is the main anti-ship missile, which is used by the Dutch Navy. It is a sea-skimming missile with a range of 124kms, at a speed of 537mph. The 488lb warhead is contact detonation. The ship launched and sub-launched variants are 4.6 metres long, due to the extra rocket booster that is used for the initial launching. The air-launched variant is 3.8 metres long, as no rocket booster is needed for launching.

[105]"RIM-66" surface-to-air missile

PD-USGOV-MILITARY-NAVY

This is the Dutch Navy's primary long-range surface-to-air missile. It is 4.72 metres long and has a range of 40 to 167kms, depending if a "first stage" booster is fitted. The missile accelerates to a speed of mach 3.5, to a maximum service ceiling of 80,000 feet. It has both infrared and semi-active terminal homing, to acquire its target. It was initially fired from surface mounted launchers, using bulky reloading systems. These have now been replaced by Vertical Launch Systems, which save weight and space, which have been deployed on newer frigates.

[104] Source http://commons.wikimedia.org/wiki/File:USS_Lawrence_(DDG_4)_launching_a_RGM-84A_Harpoon.jpg
[105] Source http://commons.wikimedia.org/wiki/File:Sm2-Launch-USN.jpg

Lightweight Torpedoes

[106]"Mark 46 Torpedo"
US Navy/MCS John L Beeman

The "Mark 46" torpedo is the standard lightweight, ship launched torpedo of the Dutch Navy. It is 2.59m in length and 324mm in diameter. It has a speed of 40knots and a range of 11 kilometres. On board ship, it is usually fired from triple torpedo tubes. Most large Dutch surface vessels carry this weapon. Helicopters are also capable of deploying this torpedo.

Heavyweight Torpedo

[107]"Mk 48"
US Navy

This heavyweight torpedo is of US origin and is deployed on the "Walrus" class of submarine. It has been in service since 2012, having been upgraded from earlier models. It is 5.79 metres long and 533mm in diameter. It can carry a 650 lb warhead 23 miles at a speed of 55 knots.

---

[106] Source http://commons.wikimedia.org/wiki/File:MK46_torpedo_launch.jpg
[107] Source http://commons.wikimedia.org/wiki/File:Mk_48_torpedo_maintenance_1982.JPEG

THE MODERN DANISH NAVY

INTRODUCTION

The Danish Navy is one of the oldest in the world. It was established in 1509, when Denmark was united with Norway. When Denmark and Norway parted company in 1814, the navy has gradually reduced in size due to government policy. The 20th Century was a century of mixed fortunes for the Danish Navy. The interwar years saw it grow to quite a force on the European stage. Unfortunately, the Second World War reversed this and the navy was almost gone by the time the war ended. In 1949, thanks to American aid, the navy was rebuilt and Denmark became one of the first members of NATO. Most of her ships would come from British and American war surplus and from captured German vessels.

The Cold War gave the Navy an easy direction to focus its efforts. It began to build vessels, which could directly challenge the Soviet Baltic Sea fleet. Mine sweepers, patrol boats and small or medium sized frigates were the order of the day. For forty years, the navy's fleet looked the same. Since the Cold War ended in 1989, the navy has had to rethink almost everything about the size and structure of its force. The enemy is now all around the world and not just in one place. The early part of this century has seen the world change and navies have had to change with it. Most operations are being conducted in the Mediterranean Sea and in the Indian Ocean. The Danish government has made the decision to keep up with these changes and are gradually building a navy to meet these new challenges.

They have focused on the surface fleet and have dispensed with the submarine force altogether. The very latest "Iver Huitfeldt" class of frigate and the "Absalon" class of frigate/support ship, fit into the long-range deployments category, which these vessels are required to do now. Whether more of these will be built remains to be seen, as the light frigates of the "Thetis" class are fast approaching the end of their service lives.

The older patrol boats have been progressively replaced by new craft and there are enough to patrol Greenland and the Arctic Circle. These craft are also more than capable to be deployed east of Suez to deal with pirate activity off Somalia.

The Danish navy is not what it was during the Cold War, but nor is any other nation's navy. It is doing its best to keep to its NATO obligations and is also doing its best with the longer-range Indian Ocean operations. No one can say that the Danish Navy isn't pulling its weight.

Pennant Numbers

Ship	Pennant Number	Ship	Pennant Number
Frigates		**Support/Frigate**	
Iver Huitfeldt	F361	Absalon	L16
Peter Willemoes	F362	Esbern Snare	L17
Niels Juel	F363		
		Ice Breakers	
Light Frigates		Danbjorn	A551
Thetis	F357	Isbjorn	A552
Triton	F358		
Vardderen	F359	**Environmental**	
Hvidbjornen	F360	**Protection Ships**	
		Gunnar Thorson	A560
Patrol Boats		Gunnar Seidenfaden	A561
Diana	P520	Mette Miljo	A562
Freja	P521	Marie Miljo	A563
Havfruen	P522		
Najaden	P523	**Training Ships**	
Nymfen	P524	Ertholm	A543
Roat	P525	Alholm	A544
Knud Rasmussen	P570	Svanen	Y101
Ejnar Mikkelsen	P571	Thyra	Y102
*	P572		
		Survey Ships	
Transport Ship		Birkholm	A541
Sleipner	A559	Fyrholm	A542
Royal Yacht		**Museum Ship**	
Dannebrog	A540	Peder Skram	F352

*still under construction

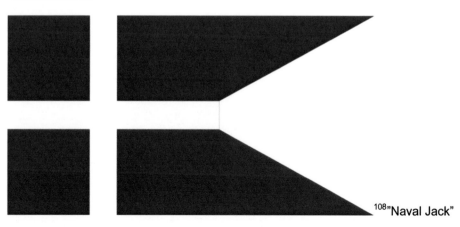

[108]"Naval Jack"

Frigates

"Iver Huidfeldt" class

[109]"Iver Huitfeldt"   Mtlarsen

Name	Pennant	Completed	Builder
Iver Huitfeldt	F361	2011	Odense Staalskibsvaerft
Peter Willemoes	F362	2011	Odense Staalskibsvaerft
Niels Juel	F363	2011	Odense Staalskibsvaerft

Displacement. 6,645 tonnes   **Dimensions.** 138.7m x 19.75m x 5.3m
Speed. 28 knots   **Complement.** 101
Armament. 2 x 76mm Oto Melara guns; 8 x Harpoon SSM; 2 x twin torpedo tubes;
4 x Mk41 8 cell VLS; 2 x Mk56 12 cell VLS; 1 x 35mm Oerlikon CIWS
Aircraft. 1 x ASW Helicopter

Notes
These three vessels are the replacements for the "Niels Juel" class of frigate. There was to have been four of these vessels, but budget restrictions reduced this to three. These frigates and the "Absalon" class support ships have transformed the Danish fleet from a coastal force to a blue water navy. The frigates were based on the

[109] Source http://commons.wikimedia.org/wiki/File:F361_Iver_Huitfeldt.jpg?uselang=en-gb

"Absalon" class, with many systems being bought "off the shelf". The ships were built to a civilian standard to minimise costs.

The ships mount an impressive weapon suite, which can be increased very easily if the situation calls for it. The forward 76mm gun can be replaced by a 127mm gun and 16 Harpoons can be embarked instead of eight. The Mk41 VLS houses the "SM-2" medium-range SAM, while the Mk56 VLS houses the "Evolved Sea Sparrow" missile. A "Westland Lynx" is currently embarked, but this will be replaced by either a "MH-60" Seahawk or an "NH-90". The complement is 101 personnel, but there is accommodation for 165 in an emergency. For last-ditch self-defence, the "Oto Melara 35mm" gun was chosen.

In 2012, "Iver Huitfeldt" operated for ten months in the Indian Ocean as part of operation "Ocean Shield", to counter Somali pirate activity.

[110]"Peter Willemoes"   MKFI

"Thetis" class

[111]"Vaedderen"   USCG/Connie Terrell

Name	Pennant	Completed	Builder
Thetis	F357	1991	Svenborg Skibsvaerft
Triton	F358	1991	Svenborg Skibsvaerft
Vaedderen	F359	1992	Svenborg Skibsvaerft
Hvidbjornen	F360	1992	Svenborg Skibsvaerft

Displacement. 3,500 tonnes   **Dimensions.** 112.3m x 14.4m x 6m
Speed. 21.8 knots   **Complement.** 60
Armament. 1 x 76mm Oto Melara gun; 7 x 12.7mm Machine guns;
          4 x 7.62mm machine guns; Depth charges and anti-submarine
          torpedoes.
Aircraft. 1 x ASW Helicopter

Notes
These light frigates were designed and built to patrol Denmark's sovereign territory of
Greenland and the Faroe Islands. Their duties are general policing, search and
rescue and fishery protection.
Due the arctic conditions, which these ships were designed for, they have been built
with an extra thick steel hull, allowing them to operate in the harshest of
environments where ice is present. They have been constantly updated and have
been fitted with extra machine guns for leaser threats. There is a large helicopter
deck to the stern with a hangar and support facilities. A "Westland Lynx" is currently

---

[111] Source http://commons.wikimedia.org/wiki/File:HDMS_Vaedderen_(F359).jpg

embarked, but this is due to be replaced by either an "MH-60" Seahawk or an "NH-90".

These vessels have proved ideal to be deployed to the Indian Ocean to participate in anti-piracy operations off Somalia. In 2008, "Thetis" served as a protection vessel for chartered ships of the World Food Organisation around the Horn of Africa region. It remains to be seen if any of the other vessels in this class will be sent East of Suez.

[112]"Thetis"   heb

[112] Source https://commons.wikimedia.org/wiki/File:RDN_F357_Thetis.jpg?uselang=en-gb

Support Ship/Frigate

"Absalon" class

[113]"Absalon"   Kim Storm Martin

Name	Pennant	Completed	Builder
Absalon	L16	2004	Odense Staalskibsvaerft
Esbern Snare	L17	2005	Odense Staalskibsvaerft

Displacement. 6,600 tonnes   **Dimensions.** 137m x 19.5m x 6.3m
Speed. 24 knots   **Complement.** 100
Armament. 1 x 127mm/54 compact gun; 7 x 12.7mm Machine guns;
    2 x 35mm Oerlikon CIWS; 2 x twin torpedo tubes
Aircraft. 2 x Helicopters

Notes
These unusual ships are part frigate and part replenishment ships. On the outside, they look like the "Iver Huitfeldt" class frigates, but on the inside, the arrangement is very different.
There is a multipurpose deck, which is accessed via a stern vehicle ramp. The deck can be used to park vehicles or other types of stores or ammunition. Mines and mine detecting equipment can also be carried and deployed. The rear vehicle ramp can also deploy and recover fast rigid boats and landing craft. A force of two hundred marines can be embarked, with equipment and put ashore.

---

[113] Source http://commons.wikimedia.org/wiki/File:L16_Absalon_with_Lynx.jpg?uselang=en-gb

The multipurpose deck is also capable of taking a containerised hospital and all support equipment to operate as a hospital ship. The ships can serve as a flagship for an admiral and seventy-five of his staff, with again, containerised command and control rooms.

Extra weapons can also be added, depending upon mission requirements. Three, twelve cell Vertical Launch tubes and eight Harpoon anti-ship missiles can be added to the mid-ship space behind the bridge superstructure. Two helicopters are usually embarked, but the type usually depends upon the mission.

[114]"Absalon"

heb

[114] Source http://commons.wikimedia.org/wiki/File:Absalon_-_20090416.jpg?uselang=en-gb

Patrol Boats

"Knud Rasmussen" class

[115]"Knud Rasmussen"

USCG/George Degener

Name	Pennant	Completed	Builder
Knud Rasmussen	P570	2008	Karstensens Skibsvaerft
Ejnar Mikkelsen	P571	2009	Karstensens Skibsvaerft
	P572	Expected 2016	Karstensens Skibsvaerft

Displacement. 2,050 tonnes   **Dimensions.** 71.8m x 14.6m x 4.9m
Speed. 17 knots   **Complement.** 43 max
Armament. 1 x 76mm gun; 2 x 12.7mm Machine guns;
      RIM-162 ESSM VLS; Anti-submarine torpedo tubes

Notes
This class of large patrol boat have been designed and built to replace the three vessels of the "Agdlek" class patrol boat. Two were initially ordered, with the third being put on hold. In 2013, the third and final vessel was ordered to replace the "Tulugaq Y388".
They have been designed to patrol the arctic waters around Greenland and Arctic Circle. The hull of the vessels has been built using thick steel for ice breaking if

[115] Source
http://commons.wikimedia.org/wiki/File:Royal_Danish_Naval_Vessel_Knut_Rasmussen_participates_in_Operation_Nanook_20
10.jpg?uselang=en-gb

necessary. The vessel main duties are fishery protection, environmental protection, search and rescue, general policing and towing and salvage.

The weapon systems on board these ships have been designed to be easily replaced or added too, if and when the mission requires. There is a large helicopter flight deck at the stern of these ships, but no hangar or support facilities are embarked.

Two fast rigid patrol boats are carried for search and seizure operations.

These vessels are well suited for operations in the Indian Ocean, but it remains to be seen whether they will be deployed east of Suez.

[116]"Knud Rasmussen"

Flemming Sorensen

[116] Source http://commons.wikimedia.org/wiki/File:P570_Knud_Rasmussen.jpg?uselang=en-gb

"Diana" class

[117]"Nymfen"   Mtlarsen

Name	Pennant	Completed	Builder
Diana	P520	2007	Faasborg Vaerft A/S
Freja	P521	2008	Faasborg Vaerft A/S
Havfruen	P522	2008	Faasborg Vaerft A/S
Najaden	P523	2008	Faasborg Vaerft A/S
Nymfen	P524	2009	Faasborg Vaerft A/S
Rota	P525	2009	Faasborg Vaerft A/S

Displacement. 246 tonnes   **Dimensions.** 43m x 8.2m x 2m
Speed. 25 knots   **Complement.** 12
Armament. 2 x 12.7mm Machine guns

Notes
This class of patrol boat was built to replace the "Barso" class of patrol boats. Their main area of operation is in Denmark's territorial waters in the Baltic Sea and the North Sea.
The vessels are tasked with general policing, search and rescue, search and seizure, environmental protection and pollution control. They also have the ability to offer divers that are in trouble a decompression chamber. The vessels can accommodate a "Stan Flex", module container depending upon the mission.

---

[117] Source http://commons.wikimedia.org/wiki/File:Nymfen.jpg?uselang=en-gb

A fast rigid boat is carried to board and inspect other vessels. The vessel are cleared to operate in icy waters of the Baltic, thanks to the reinforce hull.
The "Rota" has been used to test and evaluate a Catalyst Converter for these vessels. The test proved a great success and the class is due to have this system when they are refitted.

[118]"Najaden"   Mtlarsen

[118] Source http://commons.wikimedia.org/wiki/File:P523najaden.jpg?uselang=en-gb

Ice Breakers

"Danbjorn" class

[119]"Danbjorn", "Isbjorn" and "Thorbjorn"

Jan Beinersdorf

Name	Pennant	Completed	Builder
Danbjorn	A551	1965	Odense Staalskibsvaerft
Isbjorn	A552	1966	Odense Staalskibsvaerft

Displacement. 3,685 tonnes
Speed. 18 knots

Dimensions. 76.8m x 17.1m x 8m
Complement. 25

Notes
"Danbjorn" was acquired by the navy in 1996. When she was built, she was operated by a civilian authority but crew by the navy. In 1996, she officially became navy property.
Their duties are to keep the ports and sea-lanes around Denmark free of ice to allow shipping free movement.

---

[119] Source
http://commons.wikimedia.org/wiki/File:Ice_breakers_Danbj%C3%B8rn,_Isbj%C3%B8rn_and_Thorbj%C3%B8rn_in_Frederiksh
avn.jpg

Environmental Protection Ships

"Gunnar Thorson" class

[120]"Gunnar Thorson"

Angelbo

Name	Pennant	Completed	Builder
Gunnar Thorson	A560	1981	Orskov Christensen Staalskibsvaerft
Gunnar Seidenfaden	A561	1981	Orskov Christensen Staalskibsvaerft

Displacement. 1,660 tonnes
Speed. 12 knots

Dimensions. 55.6m x 12.3m x 4.6m
Complement. 16

Notes
These two vessels were built for the Ministry of the Environment, but were always manned by naval personnel. Both ships were transferred to the navy in 1996.

"Sea-Truck" class

[121]"Marie Miljo"

Mtlarsen

Name	Pennant	Completed	Builder
Mette Miljo	A562	1979	Nykobing Boatyard
Marie Miljo	A563	1979	Nykobing Boatyard

Displacement. 247 tonnes
Speed. 9 knots

Dimensions. 29.75m x 8.02m x 2.38m
Complement. 6

Notes
These two vessels were built for the Ministry of the Environment, but were always manned by naval personnel. Both ships were transferred to the navy in 1996.

---

[121] Source http://commons.wikimedia.org/wiki/File:Marie_Miljoe_in_kors%C3%B8r.JPG

Training Ship

"Holm" class

[122]"Ertholm"

Mtlarsen

Name	Pennant	Completed	Builder
Ertholm	A543	2006	Danish Yacht
Alholm	A544	2007	Danish Yacht

Displacement. 98 tonnes
Speed. 11 knots

Dimensions. 28.9m x 6.4m x 1.8m
Complement. 5

Notes
These training vessels usually embark four cadets at a time to teach basic
seamanship, navigation and life at sea.

[122] Source http://commons.wikimedia.org/wiki/File:A543-ertholm.JPG

"Svanen" class

123"Thyra"

Allan J Kortsen

Name	Pennant	Completed	Builder
Svanen	Y101	1960	Hundestad Boatyard
Thyra	Y102	1961	Hundestad Boatyard

Displacement. 32 tonnes
Speed. 12 knots

Dimensions. 18.8m x 4.4m x 2.4m
Complement. 4

Notes
These training vessels usually embark six cadets at a time to teach basic seamanship, navigation and life at sea.

Royal Yacht

"Dannebrog" class

[124]"Dannebrog"   Erik Christensen

Name	Pennant	Completed	Builder
Dannebrog	A540	1932	St. W. Kopenhagen

Displacement. 1,238 tonnes   **Dimensions.** 78.43m x 10.4m x 3.62m
Speed. 13.5 knots   **Complement.** 52

Notes
The Royal Yacht is the "show boat" of the Danish Navy. It serves as the official residence of the Danish Royal family when they are on overseas visits. During time of war or emergencies, she can act as a hospital ship. In 1981, she was given a refit to enable her to operate well into the next century. Considering her age, she is still in very good condition.

[124] Source http://commons.wikimedia.org/wiki/File:Royal_Danish_ship_Dannebrog_in_Vagur,_Faroe_Islands.jpg

Survey Ships

"Holm" class

"Birkholm"

Rudi Hansen

Name	Pennant	Completed	Builder
Birkholm	A541	2007	Danish Yacht
Fyrholm	A542	2006	Danish Yacht

Displacement. 98 tonnes   **Dimensions.** 28.9m x 6.4m x 1.8m
Speed. 11 knots   **Complement.** 5

Notes
These vessels were built to a common design, but were fitted for survey and seabed
mapping around Denmark's home and Arctic regions.

Transport Ship

"Sleipner" class

[126]"Sleipner"

US Navy/MCS Amanda S Kitchner

Name	Pennant	Completed	Builder
Sleipner	A559	1986	Aabenraa Shipyard

Displacement. 465 tonnes   **Dimensions.** 36.5m x 7.6m x 2.7m
Speed. 9 knots   **Complement.** 9

Notes
The "Sleipner" is the Danish Navy's only dedicated transport vessel. She was built to carry torpedoes and other munitions. These days she carries "Stan Flex" containers, ammunition and other none lethal cargos.

Museum Ship

"Peder Skram" class

[127]"Peder Skram"   Alf van Beem

Name	Pennant	Completed	Builder
Peder Skram	F352	1967	Helsingor Skibsvaerft og Maskinbyggeri A/S

Displacement. 2,200 tonnes   **Dimensions.** 112.6m x 12m x 4.3m
Speed. 28 knots   **Complement.** 180
Armament. 2 x 5inch guns; 4 x 40mm Bofors; 4 x 21inch torpedo tubes
            8 x Harpoon; 1 x Octuple Sea Sparrow SAM

Notes
The "Peder Skram" was the lead vessel in a two-ship class of frigates. Her sister ship "Herluf Trolle F353", was decommissioned in 1990 and scrapped in 1995. "Peder Skram" was also decommissioned in 1990 and was chosen to be a museum ship and moored at Copenhagen, where she is open to the public.

---

[127] Source https://commons.wikimedia.org/wiki/File:HDMS_Peder_Skram_(F352)_pic2.JPG?uselang=en-gb

Naval Aviation

"Westland Lynx"

128"Lynx"   heb

Role. Anti-submarine & Search & Rescue
Engines. 2 x Rolls-Royce Gem turboshafts
Length. 15.24m   **Rotor Diameter.** 12.8m   **Height.** 3.76m
Max Weight. 11,750lbs   **Range.** 328 miles
Max Speed. 201 mph   **Service Ceiling.** 8,540 feet
Crew. 2-3
Armament. 2 x Torpedoes, 4 x Anti-ship missiles

Notes
The Lynx entered service in 1979 and is still in service today.
It is a joint Anglo-French aircraft with Westland, (Britain), producing 70% of the
aircraft and Aerospatiale, (France), producing the remaining 30%. It is without doubt
one of the best helicopters in service anywhere in the world. To date, 13 nations still
operate the Lynx. In 2006, the Lynx Wildcat began to be developed. Danish "Lynx's"
are to be replaced by the "MH-60" Seahawk.

---

128 Source http://commons.wikimedia.org/wiki/File:Lynx_der_lander.jpg

"MH-60R"

[129]"Seahawk"   US Navy

Role. Anti-submarine & Search & Rescue
Engines. 2 x General Electric T700-GE-401C turboshafts
Length. 19.75m   **Rotor Diameter.** 16.35m   **Height.** 5.2m
Max Weight. 9,927 kgs   **Range.** 518 miles
Max Speed. 168 mph   **Service Ceiling.** 12,000 feet
Crew. 3-4
Armament. Torpedoes, Anti-ship missiles and various machine guns.

Notes
This particular variant of the very successful "Seahawk" helicopter was first flown in 1999. It has the capability to perform a variety of tasks ranging from search and rescue to hunting submarines. The Danish Navy has nine on order to replace the "Westland Lynx" from the year 2016.

[129] Source http://commons.wikimedia.org/wiki/File:MH-60R.jpg

Guns

[130]127/54 Otobreda Compact gun

This dual-purpose artillery weapon can fire various types of ammunition. It is a 5-inch gun with a ready-to-fire magazine of 66 rounds. It can fire 40 rounds per minute, to a range of 30 kms. The gun barrel is water-cooled. This weapon is gradually being replaced by the 127/64, in newer vessels.

[131]"12,7mm Browning Machine Gun"

This powerful Machine Gun is used by almost every nation in the world. It combines high fire rate (1,200 rounds per minute), long range, accuracy and sheer stopping power. It is used on most smaller warships. More are being deployed on larger warships to counter pirate attacks. It is also used in some Maritime patrol Helicopters.

[130] Source http://commons.wikimedia.org/wiki/File:Otobreda_127.54_Compact_on_ARV_Mariscal_Sucre_(F-21)_-_1987.jpg
[131] Source http://en.wikipedia.org/wiki/M2_Browning_machine_gun

[132]"AA 52 7.62mm Machine Gun"

Jean-Michel Roche

This machine gun is used by almost all of the armed forces in the world. As a general-purpose machine gun, it can be used and deployed anywhere. It is mainly deployed on smaller craft and patrol boats of the Danish Navy. It is now being deployed on larger vessels to counter pirate attacks.

[133]"76mm gun"

User:STB-1

Developed by the Italian company Oto Melara, the 76mm Super Rapid has become somewhat of a standard when it comes to putting maximum firepower in a smaller calibre artillery piece. It is capable of fitting into most of the smaller type of naval vessels, such as patrol boats, corvettes and sloops. The rate of fire is impressive, with 120 rounds per minute. The gun's high rate of fire and availability of specialized ammunition make it well suited in varied roles such as short-range anti-missile point defence, anti-aircraft, anti-surface, and ground support. Specialized ammunition includes armour piercing, incendiary, directed fragmentation effects, and a guided round marketed as capable of destroying incoming missiles.

[132] Source http://en.wikipedia.org/wiki/AA-52_machine_gun#mediaviewer/File:Motte-Picquet-ANF1.jpg
[133] Source http://commons.wikimedia.org/wiki/File:76mm_gun_chikuma.JPG?uselang=en-gb

[134]"Oerlikon 35mm gun.

CraigWyllie

This weapon is now beginning to make its mark on the world market. Denmark and Turkey are the only countries so far to deploy this weapon on it their ship. It can fire 1000 rounds per minute, out to an effective range of 3,500 metres. The ammunition can be contact or proximity burst.

Missiles

[135]"RIM-162" ESSM

US Navy/MCS Matthew J Haran

The "RIM-162" is the Vertical Launch upgrade of the "RIM-7" missile. A larger more powerful engine is required because the missile is vertically launched. This also allows the missile to have an extended range of 50kms at a speed of mach 4. It is housed in the VLS "Mk 41" launcher. This is a four-missile canister, which can be deployed on smaller vessels, not just larger destroyers. The "Mk 48" launcher is a two-missile canister, for even smaller vessels.

---

[134] Source
http://commons.wikimedia.org/wiki/File:Oerlikon_Millennium_35_mm_Naval_Revolver_Gun_Systems_on_HDMS_Absalon_(L16).jpg?uselang=en-gb
[135] Source http://commons.wikimedia.org/wiki/File:RIM-162_ESSM_launched_from_USS_Carl_Vinson.jpg?uselang=en-gb

[136]"Harpoon" anti-ship missile

US Navy/MCS Kevin V Cunningham

The "Harpoon" is the main anti-ship missile, which is used by the Danish Navy. It is a sea-skimming missile with a range of 124kms, at a speed of 537mph. The 488lb warhead is contact detonation. The ship launched and sub-launched variants are 4.6 metres long, due to the extra rocket booster that is used for the initial launching. The air-launched variant is 3.8 metres long, as no rocket booster is needed for launching.

[137]"RIM-66" surface-to-air missile

PD-USGOV-MILITARY-NAVY

This is the Danish Navy's primary long-range surface-to-air missile. It is 4.72 metres long and has a range of 40 to 167kms, depending if a "first stage" booster is fitted. The missile accelerates to a speed of mach 3.5, to a maximum service ceiling of 80,000 feet. It has both infrared and semi-active terminal homing, to acquire its target. It was initially fired from surface mounted launchers, using bulky reloading systems. These have now been replaced by Vertical Launch Systems, which save weight and space, which have been deployed on newer frigates.

[136] Source http://commons.wikimedia.org/wiki/File:Harpoon_missile_launch_aboard_USS_Shiloh.jpg
[137] Source http://commons.wikimedia.org/wiki/File:Sm2-Launch-USN.jpg

Lightweight Torpedo

[138]"MU-90" torpedo

Causa83

Originally developed in the 1980's as a joint project between France and Italy, it wasn't until the 1990's that production began.

Weighting 304 kgs at a length of 2.85metres and a diameter of 323.7mm, this torpedo is capable of being fired from a ship or aircraft. It has a range of 5 to 12 miles depending on its speed of 50 knots maximum, with its pump-jet propulsion. The warhead is a shape charge weighting 32.7 kgs.

[138] Source http://commons.wikimedia.org/wiki/File:MU90_torpedo_01.jpg?uselang=en-gb